AF147182

On Theory-Fiction and Other Genres

Simon O'Sullivan

On Theory-Fiction and Other Genres

palgrave
macmillan

Simon O'Sullivan
Visual Cultures
Goldsmiths
London, UK

ISBN 978-3-031-65071-0   ISBN 978-3-031-65072-7   (eBook)
https://doi.org/10.1007/978-3-031-65072-7

© The Editor(s) (if applicable) and The Author(s), under exclusive license to Springer Nature Switzerland AG 2024

This work is subject to copyright. All rights are solely and exclusively licensed by the Publisher, whether the whole or part of the material is concerned, specifically the rights of translation, reprinting, reuse of illustrations, recitation, broadcasting, reproduction on microfilms or in any other physical way, and transmission or information storage and retrieval, electronic adaptation, computer software, or by similar or dissimilar methodology now known or hereafter developed.
The use of general descriptive names, registered names, trademarks, service marks, etc. in this publication does not imply, even in the absence of a specific statement, that such names are exempt from the relevant protective laws and regulations and therefore free for general use.
The publisher, the authors and the editors are safe to assume that the advice and information in this book are believed to be true and accurate at the date of publication. Neither the publisher nor the authors or the editors give a warranty, expressed or implied, with respect to the material contained herein or for any errors or omissions that may have been made. The publisher remains neutral with regard to jurisdictional claims in published maps and institutional affiliations.

This Palgrave Macmillan imprint is published by the registered company Springer Nature Switzerland AG.
The registered company address is: Gewerbestrasse 11, 6330 Cham, Switzerland

If disposing of this product, please recycle the paper.

For my students at Goldsmiths, past and present

Prelude

Her unblinking eyes were of a deep cobalt blue. She held out a fist to me, rotated her wrist and slowly uncurled her fingers. On the palm of her hand were a collection of glass-like objects of different shapes and sizes. Looking at them there, they didn't appear natural, but cut and ground with precision and care. One by one she carefully picked them up between the thumb and forefinger of her other hand, holding them in turn so they were level with both her eyes and mine. Each of them caught the light in different ways. There were prisms that separated out the light into a kaleidoscope of different colours. Lenses that focused the light or bent it somehow. And then there were other lenses that were more opaque or clouded over. The small, mirrored objects that she also held up reflected back not just her face, but mine too, as well as the other details of our surroundings. Depending on how they were held these mirrors also appeared as if they were holes within the world. There were also objects that seemed to be both prisms and mirrors, depending on how she turned them in her fingers and positioned them in front of my eyes. Finally there were the sparkling crystals—*so many!*— each unique and with a different number of angled faces. All of different colours and reflecting and mirroring the light in a myriad of ways. It was difficult to understand how these might be used or, indeed, what they *were* exactly (although when I squinted my eyes or turned my head slightly it was as if they showed some other world—suddenly present and vivid—that had always been there but obscured). I had the sense that I was being shown a series of optical devices, not to choose one exactly, but so as to grasp that there were, indeed, different options and perspectives, and further, seeing them there held up to my face, that my own eyes and hers too might themselves be understood as just further sets of these devices that were also here, now, on display.

Acknowledgements

Thanks to Jon K Shaw for his insightful comments and editorial suggestions on an early draft of this book and for his careful and astute proofreading; Tom O'Sullivan for conversations around art writing and for comments on a draft of the chapter on art writing; Ola Ståhl for conversations around writing and for our own writing collaborations; the two anonymous reviewers at Palgrave for their comments on a later draft and for encouraging publication; the MA Contemporary Art students at Goldsmiths who took my seminar 'From Art Writing to Theory-Fiction' from 2020 to 2023 and 'On Theory-Fiction and Other Genres' in 2023 and whose conversations have fed into this book; and Brendan George and everyone at Palgrave and Newgen for making the publication process so smooth and swift.

Contents

1

Introduction: Three Genres

Abstract In my short Introduction, I introduce the three different kinds of writing practice—theory-fiction, autofiction and autotheory, and art writing—that the following essays concern themselves with. In particular, I briefly lay out some of my provisional argument that these forms of writing not only enact a blurring between genres but also are each performative in some manner. I also introduce the question of place (and circuits) of publication and dissemination of these 'new' kinds of writing. This relates not only to what has become known as para-academia (especially as regards theory-fiction) but also to the growth in small presses (especially for art writing). My Introduction also briefly addresses how these 'new' forms of writing involve a turn away not only from more typical academic or essayistic writing but also from literary fiction per se (having closer connections to what is sometimes called 'genre fiction'). It is this position in the margins—and away from at least some gatekeepers— that also means these 'new' genres can speak about other experiences and other subject positions.

Keywords Theory-Fiction • Autofiction • Autotheory • Art Writing • Machine Writing • Hybrid Genres

© The Author(s), under exclusive license to Springer Nature Switzerland AG 2024   1
S. O'Sullivan, *On Theory-Fiction and Other Genres*,
https://doi.org/10.1007/978-3-031-65072-7_1

In the following three essays, I look at three different kinds of writing practice—theory-fiction, autofiction and autotheory, and art writing—that are increasingly prevalent as genres—or 'hybrid genres'—in the critical humanities. In fact, it is only the first two essays that can be accurately described as such: the third really concerns contemporary art practice and looks to a mode of writing—often involving other registers besides language—that is prevalent there. As well as anything else, each of the essays operates as a brief critical survey of these 'new' forms of writing—many examples are listed, especially in my footnotes—whilst at the same time, they work towards some provisional definitions. I also identify some precursors. More importantly, however, is that I attempt to work out what these 'new' kinds of writing do. What is particular to them or what do they add to those already existing styles and genres (and especially the academic essay, article and book)? In a postscript to the essays—and on a slight tangent to them—I then also briefly turn to Artificial Intelligence (AI) text production systems or what I call 'machine writing'. What is the implication of the latter for genre and for writing more generally? In terms of their length and breadth, the essays on theory-fiction and art writing are longer and attempt to cover more ground, whilst the two on autowriting and machine writing are shorter and operate more as interventions into their respective fields.

I should say from the start that my account is partial and dictated by my own location in London and the UK and familiarity with a certain scene of writing. The area of hybrid and cross-genre writing is increasing in size, to say nothing of those other forms of experimental writing that dovetail with some of the genres my book explores. Certainly other trajectories could be plotted and other definitions put forward.[1] To a large extent, the texts I mention in my essays are those which I have found or which have found me (see my coda to the first essay for a more subjective account of a particular scene of writing that determined some of my take on theory-fiction, for example).[2]

To jump ahead a little, the argument throughout my book is generally that these new modes of writing, as well as often tackling urgent issues, perform their content in some manner (in terms of being both related to performance *and* operating as a performative utterance). It is also in this sense that I sometimes figure these modes/genres of writing as different kinds of device that allow this performing of content, especially in rela-tion to a switching or shuttling of perspective. This takes different forms. For example, with theory-fiction, there is a *fictioning* of theory, if I can put it like that; or, put slightly differently, there is a dramatising of con-ceptual resources. Theory-fiction can also involve the offering up of dif-ferent perspectives and even, I would suggest, the expression of other modes of existence (which is why it can be such an appropriate form of writing in terms of addressing the issues of the Anthropocene). Autowriting, as well as being writing that brings the author as character into a fiction (with autofiction) or relating theory to an actual lived life (with autotheory)—especially when such authors are marked and mar-ginalised (hence the importance of women's writing and trans experi-ences in this writing)—can also involve the framing of what I have elsewhere called the 'fiction of the self'.[3] Put differently, autowriting allows a reflection on the self as *already* a fiction that is written and, in some senses, performed. This has important implications for any project of self-transformation—something I will return to (in terms of my own investments in this project) in a final coda to my book—or indeed for our general sense of being and becoming in the world. As I mentioned above, art writing moves between registers and genres and also in many ways more obviously performs its content (which is why it has such strong resonances with literary experimentation). It can also play with ideas of authorship, inventing authors or otherwise foregrounding the importance of different scenes and communities—or involving collabo-rations with both human and non-human agents (as is also the case, for example, with machine writing and our collaborations with AI). Finally, there is a sense with all these different kinds of writing that there is a blur-ring not only between different genres but also between fiction and real-ity. In fact, it is also the case that some of this writing—in the case of theory-fiction—works to bring about its own reality (it involves a strange retro-causality where the fiction works back on its conditions of emergence).

As well as these questions of style and genre—and the more radical time looping I just mentioned—there is also the question of place (and circuits) of publication and dissemination of these new kinds of writing. This relates not only to what has become known as para-academia (especially as regards theory-fiction) but also to the growth in small presses (especially for art writing) and, more generally, the continuing use of and experimentation with the book form (a particularly interesting phenomenon in the light of ubiquitous digitisation and the web, something that has also had an effect on these new kinds of writing). I go into this more in the essays 'On Theory-Fiction' and 'On Art Writing', but to jump ahead again, it does seem as if these new forms of writing are located in a kind of borderland, away from more typical academic or essayistic writing—and Philosophy with a capital 'P'—but also away from more typical literary fiction (having closer connections to what is known as 'genre fiction'). It is this position in the margins—and away from at least some gatekeepers—that also means this writing can speak about other experiences and from other subject positions (which is why I think it has a particular contribution to make towards the project of decolonisation, something I address in a coda to my third essay). It is also in this sense that these new forms of writing represent what might be called a democratisation of theory (and of the literary too, at least in some senses). There is certainly a sense that theory-fiction and other new genres are re-opening a space or field of the commons. These new genres of writing are both from and for different communities. Or, put differently, they are devices that are involved in proliferating different and diverse *scenes* of writing.[4]

Notes

1. See, for example, Nick Thoburn's *Anti-Book* for an account of experimental writing (and the book form) in relation to radical politics (2016). Thoburn also makes many astute remarks about the artist's book (or 'bookwork'), defined by Thoburn as 'a mode of aesthetic production that takes as its object the physical, formal, and institutional qualities of the textual medium of which it is constituted' (Thoburn 2016: 9).
2. A further determining factor to mention at the outset of this small book is that I gathered the following thoughts around writing at the same time as writing a piece of theory-fiction/art writing that was also an autofiction at least of a kind (and, at times, something I thought of as an experimental novel). The process of writing that work—now published as *The Ancient*

Device (O'Sullivan 2024a)—partly dictated some of the propositions and the selection of indicative texts in what follows. Further essays written around and about writing and other art practices—and attendant general themes, some of them more personal—can be found in a further collection of essays that I wrote at the same time as those in this book: *From Magic and Myth-Work to Care and Repair* (2024b).

3. See especially the essays in the first half of my book mentioned in the footnote above (O'Sullivan 2024b).

4. In relation to scenes, I want to say at the outset that my thoughts on these different genres of writing are indebted also to the MA students at Goldsmiths that took my seminar 'From Art Writing to Theory-Fiction' during the years 2020–2023 and those that took a shorter course with me 'On Theory-Fiction and Other Genres' in 2023 (I will briefly return to the latter in a coda to my 'Autofiction and Autotheory' chapter). The experience of teaching that seminar—especially when Covid meant we had to move online—has taught me the importance of community and of how a scene (in this case of teaching) can generate work over and above any individual contributions.

References

O'Sullivan, Simon (2024a), *The Ancient Device*, Charmouth: Triarchy Press.

———— (2024b), *From Magic and Myth-Work to Care and Repair*, London: Goldsmiths Press.

Thoburn, Nick (2016), *Anti-Book: On the Art and Politics of Radical Publishing*, Minneapolis: University of Minnesota Press.

2

On Theory-Fiction

Abstract What does theory-fiction bring to theory? What does it add to it (if anything)? This essay attempts to answer these questions and is organised around ten sections, each of which makes a different set of claims, while also identifying some precursors, certain scenes of writing and other key examples of this genre. The ten sections are as follows: (1) Dramatisation and Deterritorialisation. In which I attend to theory-fiction's dramatisation of concepts, its non-philosophical character (following François Laruelle) and its operation as a kind of 'minor' writing (following Gilles Deleuze and Félix Guattari). (2) Cybernetic Theory-Fictions. Here I attend to a key scene of theory-fiction that involves Science Fiction and cybernetics. (3) Hyperstitions and Other Nestings. Following directly on from 2., this section concerns the idea of fictions making themselves real via feedback loops. (4) From Ethnopoetics to Ecopoetics. In this section, I look to other kinds of theoretical writing that also involve fiction as method. (5) Science Fictions and Sympoiesis. Here I address those theory-fictions that present non-human and inter-species perspectives. (6) Outside Perspectives and Critical Fabulations. In which I explore how theory-fiction operates as an optic to an outside or onto historical trauma. (7) Different Registers. Here I look at the way in which theory-fiction also uses other forms of representation. (8) Formal Devices. In which I turn back to writing and explore some of the more

© The Author(s), under exclusive license to Springer Nature Switzerland AG 2024
S. O'Sullivan, *On Theory-Fiction and Other Genres*,
https://doi.org/10.1007/978-3-031-65072-7_2

formal devices of theory-fiction. (9) Performing Texts. In this section I attend to the idea of texts that perform their content and that also call to be performed. (10) Sites of Production and Modes of Existence. My last section explores the idea that theory-fiction is situated away from the mainstream and thus can express other subject positions and modes of existence. In a coda to this first essay, I briefly lay out my own determining encounter with a certain scene of theory-fiction and attend briefly to the idea that a scene might itself be a theory-fiction too.

Keywords Theory-Fiction • Hyperstition • Ethnopoetics • Ecopoetics • Critical Fabulation • Fictocriticism

Dramatisation and Deterritorialisation

What does theory-fiction bring to theory?[1] What does it add to it (if anything)? On the one hand, it allows a form of dramatisation. Theory-fiction can operate as a kind of theatrical device (or as a set of such devices). It can invent characters and/or different set-ups (so, scenes and narratives) that allow concepts to be played out or 'lived', as it were. There are many precursors to the current scene here, for example, Nietzsche's Zarathustra, or Gilles Deleuze and Félix Guattari's Professor Challenger (from the 'Geology of Morals' plateau of *A Thousand Plateaus* [Deleuze and Guattari 1988: 39–74]) himself 'on loan' from Sir Arthur Conan Doyle.[2] Fiction shifts the register in this sense. It can give theory more traction on a life as it means we relate to it in a different way (after all, we are also living a life). But it also further abstracts any conceptual material away from philosophy/theory and into a world of fiction. This doubling—the fictioning of a fiction (which is one understanding of what concepts are)—rather than diluting any force can increase it. It is as if the change in context (and thus in perspective) allows something else—not least the inventive and experimental aspects of theory—to become foregrounded.

Another way of saying this is that theory-fiction—or, again, the fictioning of theory—disables what can be the arrogant operation of more philosophically orientated theory whilst at the same time increasing its combinatory powers. It drops down the particular perspective that theory—and even more particularly Philosophy (with a capital 'P')—can maintain over its purview.[3] François Laruelle's non-philosophy project might be understood as a kind of theory-fiction in these terms (or a theory of theory-fiction at least).[4] Certainly, non-philosophy partly involves a refiguring or even re-purposing of concepts—once they have been untethered from this overview and 'truth' value—as 'philo-fictions'. Following Laruelle, there is something radically democratic in this 'dropping down' or flattening procedure (a radical change in perspective). Hierarchy and a certain kind of authority is disabled and, with that, other kinds of work—perhaps more experimental?—become possible. Or again, a kind of pragmatic and combinatory logic can take over (this is what I have elsewhere called a diagrammatic logic [see O'Sullivan 2016]).

Another and perhaps more straightforward kind of theory-fiction is about blurring the distinction between theory and fiction.[5] Or demonstrating that the border has—in many cases—always already been porous. Deleuze and Guattari attend to this idea at the end of *What Is Philosophy?* (although they don't use the term theory-fiction) where all sorts of crossings and 'intrinsic' interferences between different kinds of thought are at stake. In particular—and in relation to this essay—there are those cases where aesthetic figures traverse the philosophical plane of immanence (of concept creation) or conceptual personae wander onto an aesthetic plane of composition (where blocs of affect are erected) (Deleuze and Guattari 1994: 217). These interferences would seem to characterise Deleuze and Guattari's own writings and especially *A Thousand Plateaus*, a work in which fiction is certainly as much of a resource as philosophy but which also, as I mentioned above, at times mobilises theory-fiction as one of its methods (see also O'Sullivan 2017a).

A further inflection on this—to briefly stay with Deleuze and Guattari—is that theory-fiction might be said to be a kind of 'minor' theory: 'to hate all languages of masters', as they remark in their book on the minor literature of Kafka (Deleuze and Guattari 1986: 26). Certainly, theory-fiction works to deterritorialise the major language of philosophy.[6] I have written about this idea of the minor in relation to contemporary art practice elsewhere (see O'Sullivan 2006), but it does seem to me that we could speculatively 'apply' Deleuze and Guattari's three

demarcations of the minor to theory-fiction. To be very brief and reduc-
tive: (1) It deterritorialises a major language (in this case, of theory/
Philosophy) especially in its foregrounding of affect and intensity (see
also the remarks in my coda to this essay); (2) It is always connected to
larger circuits (that is to say, it emphasises the theoretical aspect of fiction
or the way in which fiction can have an effect in and on other terrains and
regimes); and (3) It is collective in character (as in the way it is associated
with certain scenes, for example, the one I discuss in the next section).
We might also note here that theory-fiction is often mobilised by those
outside the academy or in the borderlands of the disciplines of philosophy and critical/cultural theory per se—which is to say, again, that it
turns away from, or does something to, more typical and major forms of
philosophical expression as well as their institutions and gatekeepers. I'll
return to this question of the spaces and places of production of theory-
fiction below.

Cybernetic Theory-Fictions

A contemporary work that partly looks to Deleuze and Guattari and that
uses fiction as both a resource and a method—and also explores fiction's
traction on reality more generally—is Sadie Plant's work of cyberfeminism
Zeros and Ones (1997). In particular, Plant attends to how certain Science
Fictions (especially William Gibson's *Neuromancer*) operate retroactively
'as though the present was being reeled into a future which had always
been guiding the past' (Plant 1997: 13).[7] I introduce this book here as it
seems to me to be one of the first contemporary theory-fiction works, but
also because with Plant's books and essays we have a demonstration that
this kind of writing has its precursors away from philosophy, for example
with various Situationist texts and, indeed, other counter-cultural scenes
(see also the discussions in Plant's first book *The Most Radical Gesture*
[1992]).[8] In *Zeros and Ones*, Plant pays particular attention to the impact
of 'new' technology on writing—especially hypertext—and how this, in
itself, effects what writing (and theory) is and might become (although she
also points out that Michel Foucault, for example, was already attentive to
the way writing necessarily overflows the book form).[9] *Zeros and Ones* also

involves the telling of a different story about our relationship to technology and, indeed, attends to the pivotal role of women in technological development (especially with Ada Lovelace). But, once again, it is particularly the style of Plant's writing that seems crucial, not least the way it presents Science Fiction narrative (both Plant's and that by others) alongside more historical and theoretical accounts.

We can see this Science Fiction inflected theory further in play in another key work of theory-fiction that is contemporary to *Zeros and Ones* (and part of the same scene): the 'book' *Cyberpositive* by the collective artist 0[rphan] d[rift>] (1996). Both this and Plant's book are connected to the work of the Cybernetic culture research unit (Ccru), to whom I will return below. David Burrows and I have written at length about *Cyberpositive*, especially in relation to its style and syntax and the way it seems to be not simply about the future but from it somehow—as if it had been thrown back in time (see Burrows and O'Sullivan 2019: 302–305).[10] Like *Zeros and Ones*, it is a work in which fiction and theory are tightly interwoven and one that performs its content in that its style and presentation are part of what make it so compelling (and difficult; it's certainly not an easy read). Plant's book also had an impact on subsequent writing at the intersection of feminism and technology, not least those texts that bring theory and fiction into relation, as, for example, with some of Luciana Parisi's writing (another member of the Ccru) and the more recent essays of Amy Ireland (which I will briefly return to in my postscript 'On Machine Writing').[11] A further key example of this kind of theory-fiction (and another contemporary [and pre-cursor to a certain extent] to Plant) is Donna Haraway's highly influential 'Cyborg Manifesto' (1991). This 'Science Fable', as Haraway calls it, explicitly mobilises fiction and a future perspective to make its argument about women in the integrated circuit. I will be turning to Haraway and her more recent theory-fictions below.[12]

In relation to the scene that Plant was part of, there are also the writings of Nick Land which, in the 1990s, moved from a strictly philosophical register to a more theory-fiction one.[13] I have written about these theory-fiction essays—in particular, 'Meltdown' and 'Circuitries' (Land 2011)—elsewhere (see O'Sullivan 2017b), but it's worth restating here that these texts are also key precursors to the current scene and, like Plant's, involve a turn to Science Fiction as resource, but also an account of fiction as positive feedback loop and time-travelling device (that is, as hyperstitional practice; I'll return to this below).[14] Land and Plant also collaborated on theory-fictions, such as the 1994 essay 'Cyberpositive' (and in fact, Land was also part of the 'swarm' that wrote the *Cyberpositive* book I mentioned above). More generally, both Land and Plant were interested in cybernetics and, as such, with theory-fiction that concerned itself with (and operated as) temporal circuit (the positive feedback loops I mentioned above) (Land and Plant 1994).[15] Finally, to complete the set of key precursors—in relation to these cybernetic theory-fictions—there are Mark Fisher's important writings (including his PhD) that bring the fiction of writers like J. G. Ballard into productive encounter with theorists like Jean Baudrillard (as well as Deleuze and Guattari and many others) (see Fisher 2018b). Fisher, who had Plant as PhD supervisor for a time, also attends to more popular and counter-cultural forms of theory-fiction.[16] Crucially, it was Plant who set up the Ccru that Fisher was part of, and which Land later became involved in. Like Plant, Fisher was interested in how an understanding of cybernetics changes our relation to theory and fiction ('the era of cybernetics eliminates—or smears—the distinction between theory and fiction' [Fisher 2018b: 5]). It also changes our understanding of the relationship between different times or foregrounds the possibility of transit between times. Certainly, Ballard and Baudrillard, for example, might be said to write from the future into the present. They are also situated at the edge of their respective genres (writing from fiction into theory and theory into fiction, respectively). With Fisher there is then the later reconfiguration of this time-travelling aspect of theory-fiction with the idea of hauntology and the attention he gives to those lost futures that continue to haunt the present (Fisher 2014).

Hyperstitions and Other Nestings

Following these figures and their different texts, theory-fiction might then be understood as a name for those fictions that operate theoretically or, at least, have a realm of operation beyond a strictly literary setting (so fictions that cross into other terrains and fields of operation). This includes the way fictions can insert themselves into reality, as in the Ccru's concept of 'hyperstition', defined as fictions that make themselves real and/or have real effects within a given milieu (see Ccru n.d.).[17] Or, put differently, for the Ccru, there are fictions—or hyperstitions—in which what might be called ontological borders—between fiction and reality—become blurred or in which already-present virtualities can become actualised.[18] Indeed, for the Ccru, 'reality is understood to be composed of fictions—consistent semiotic terrains that condition perceptual, affective and behaviorial responses' (Ccru 2017: 35) and, as such, this reality can itself be re-fictioned.

Related to this are the various nested fictions in the Ccru's writing. An example here is the essay 'Lemurian Time War' (Ccru 2017) in which there are multiple 'fictions within fictions' at work, not least those concerning the work and identity of the Ccru itself.[19] As I have suggested elsewhere, nesting fictions in this way does something—recursively, as it were—to our own perspective on the fiction we move in and through (if only allowing us to see the latter *as* a fiction).[20] Theory-fiction, at times, seems to involve this play of fictions within fictions and, as such, can foreground the always already fictional status of any given reality (or, indeed, of the self). I will return to this nesting or 'doubling' function below in relation to some of the other genres my own book is concerned with.

As the Ccru demonstrate in their writings—not least the essay on 'Lemurian Time War' mentioned above—there are connections here with a writer like William Burroughs, who mobilised the cut-up method as a way of slicing into existing narratives and set-ups (and, indeed, accessing an outside to the latter). Burroughs saw reality as a series of 'control' scripts that, for him (and in order to escape time), needed to be interrupted and edited. It was in this sense that writing was specifically a magical technology.[21] To quote the Ccru: 'Burroughs construed writing—and art in general—not aesthetically, but functionally—that is to say, magically, with magic defined as the use of signs to produce changes in reality' (Ccru 2017: 35). Burroughs—along with Ballard—seems like the key fiction precursor to this particular cybernetic theory-fiction scene (as, once again, demonstrated in Fisher's own theoretical exploration and critical survey [Fisher 2018b]) and to the idea of fiction having real effects.[22]

More generally—and to turn away from the Ccru (at least to a certain extent)—there are those theory-fictions that use Science Fiction tropes or involve a kind of science fictioning of theory, as with Simon Sellar's *Applied Ballardianism* (2018) or Steve Beard's *Six Concepts for the End of the World* (2019).[23] In both of these cases, the respective books are about another writer—in this case, Ballard and Paul Virilio—and use the set-up of a fiction to explore their ideas or shift the context (and, in so doing, once again, blur the border between fiction and reality). Indeed, to say it again, theory-fiction seems to be partly about this shifting of contexts or moving from one genre to another. Another recent example here is Benjamin H. Bratton's *Dispute Plan to Prevent Future Luxury Constitution*, which also moves between fiction and theory genres (2015) and, as with the Sellars and Beard books, involves a fictional narrator (or investigator) as a key device.

I want to conclude this second section of my first essay by briefly turning to theory-fictions—broadly conceived—written in collaboration with cybernetic systems or which—to some extent anyway—involve the perspective of an AI. See, for example, *Pharmako AI* (K Allado-McDowell 2020) which seems to take the logic at work in a book like *Cyberpositive* one step further (insofar as it is not a book about AI or even, in this case, a fictioned performance of it—but a real collaboration, at least to some extent).[24] It seems to me that cybernetic theory-fiction is making a leap of sorts with the increasing availability of these AI systems and associated perspectives, but also that the latter foreground the way in which theory-fiction, in some of its guises, has always disrupted any conservative idea of a single author or agent or of what any given agent actually consists (as is the case, for example, with *Cyberpositive*). A certain kind of theory-fiction has always been a writing from the future into the present in this sense. I will return more specifically to AI-generated texts in a postscript to this book 'On Machine Writing'.

From Ethnopoetics to Ecopoetics

We might also turn in a different direction—away from cybernetics and its accompanying fictions—and note theory-fiction's connection with what has been called ethnopoetics and, indeed, those other anthropological fictions that foreground a different perspective on reality (or even a perspective on different realities). Certainly, there is an increasing sense that anthropology (for example) has no more claim to truth than the cultures it writes about and, following this, that a different style of writing (from that more typically found in the social sciences) might be more appropriate to this discipline. In his essay on 'The Corn Wolf: Writing Apotropaic Texts' (2010), Michael Taussig suggests precisely this, demarcating a 'Nervous System writing' (that includes his own)—concerned, amongst other things, with 'as-ifs taken as real' (Taussig 2010: 31)—from 'agribusiness writing' that 'wants mastery' and which 'we find throughout the university' (and which would include anthropological business-as-usual) (Taussig 2010: 29). Agribusiness writing is also a specifically extractive writing practice in terms of knowledge production (an idea I will return to in the following essay).

There is also Taussig's account of 'field work' more generally and, indeed, his exploration of different kinds of writing—and other registers (drawings, diagrams and the like)—that might be mobilised in relation to any objects of study (Taussig 2011). Once again, theory-fiction—broadly understood—seems to be a way of disabling a certain kind of authority (and, in this case, any supposed mastery). Or, put differently, there is here a writing practice that is situated on the same level as the material being looked at (so, again, a kind of 'dropping down' of perspective). More generally—and here I am also gesturing towards autotheory—there is an *auto*ethnographic impulse at work in this kind of writing that invariably foregrounds the author's own subjective standpoint or situated perspective (again, see Taussig 2011). In relation to this, see also Roy Wagner's *Coyote Anthropology* (2010) that plays with reality/fiction in the kind of way Taussig suggests (as well as with foreground/background perspectives) and also proceeds by way of a theatrical set-up between Roy (the author) and Coyote (the trickster) (see the discussion of this text in Burrows and O'Sullivan 2019: 177–181). Wagner's prompt for his book are the writings of Carlos Casteneda, perhaps the ur-ethnopoetical texts and ones in which the idea of 'as-ifs taken as real' is crucial (see the discussion of Casteneda in Burrows and O'Sullivan 2019: 53–55).

A further genre (or perhaps we should call it a *field* of writing practice) connected to ethnopoetics and anthropology more generally—and one that also has a political urgency—is that of ecopoetics. Again, this can involve the inter-weaving of a more personal narrative—and/or of fiction—with any theoretical material, as, for example, with a writer like Anna Tsing, who foregrounds her subjective experience as part of the project of exploring ways of living in the ruins of capitalist extraction and other blasted landscapes (Tsing 2015). I will return to Tsing (and Taussig) in my essay on autowriting. In many ways the issues of our Anthropocene—and of the climate emergency—are linked to a certain extractive attitude and value system, which might be typified by writing that pretends an objective or disembodied view or reinforces a certain kind of subject/object split (so Taussig's 'agribusiness writing'). This is why a text like Eduardo Viveiros de Castro's *Cannibal Metaphysics* is especially important in its critique of Western anthropological models and in its laying out of a theory of 'perspectivism' (from Amerindian ontology), an idea that itself involves shuttling between points of view (Viveiros de Castro 2014). We might say that the use of theory-fiction here—as a method—is then part of the wider project of the critical eco-humanities that seeks to explore other value systems and other ways of being. Theory-fiction here is also a name for those texts that turn to story-telling themselves in order to perform this critique and, indeed, switch perspective (see, for example, Martin Savransky's exploration of 'storied worlds' in his *Around the Day in Eighty Worlds: Politics of the Pluriverse* [2021]). I will say more about storytelling in the section below and return to some of these ideas of ecopoetics in connection to decolonisation (and in relation to some examples of recent writing) in a coda to my essay 'On Art Writing'.

Science Fictions and Sympoiesis

Theory-fiction can then involve writing about different perspectives, and also, more radically, can itself offer up different perspectives too. Indeed, if autotheory and autofiction are about the self—even if this self is fragmented and fractured—then theory-fiction might be said to play around with other perspectives outside this self (although there are limits here, after all, theory-fiction is written in language).[25] Burrows and I have previously explored some of this terrain in relation to Science Fiction writing and 'Inhuman Social Imaginaries' (see Burrows and O'Sullivan 2019: 275–293), but it is worth restating here that this experimental form of theory-fiction, that involves playing with and presenting non-human perspectives, also tends towards the genre of Science Fiction insofar as it involves using fiction to invent and/or explicate concepts and experiment beyond a given set-up (and also to explore actors in networks, that is, experiment *within* a given set-up—a problem close to the anthropologist having an effect on that which they observe).[26]

This is the case in some of Donna Haraway's recent writings, which offer up a different take on theory-fiction to, for example, the cybernetic one of the Ccru and, especially, those Promethean and accelerationist stories that in many ways follow the Ccru.[27] Haraway writes about the importance of fiction as a resource for her work (in terms of theory or, more generally, for fields outside literature) as exemplified by her own turn to both the fiction and the writing on fiction of the Science Fiction/Fantasy writer Ursula Le Guin (herself brought up on anthropology).[28] But Haraway also deploys a theory-fiction method herself in order to explore non-human and inter-species perspectives (and especially what she calls 'sympoiesis'), as in the narrative that comes at the end of her book *Staying with the Trouble*, 'The Camille Stories' (see Haraway 2016: 134–168). Like some of the other texts I have already mentioned (I'm thinking here, especially of the Ccru ones, as well as Plant and Land), Haraway's *Staying with the Trouble* seems to me to have initiated a 'new' sub-genre within theory-fiction concerned precisely with multi-species storytelling and the exploration of non-human perspectives more generally.[29] Here, theory-fiction is again a dramatisation, in this case involving the invention of various figures and avatars that embody certain ideas or speculatively play them out. Haraway's theory-fiction also utilises a further device of Science Fiction, namely future projection. 'The Camille Stories' follows different generations of the non-human 'symbiont' Camille, such that the fiction allows a different temporal scale to be in play and, with that, the exploration of certain ideas—about 'how to live in the ruins' (Haraway 2016: 138)—across multiple generations. More generally, then, theory-fiction can involve the exploration and foregrounding of these different kinds of agency.[30]

Crucially however—and as I mentioned above—theory-fiction also allows a kind of doubling—or staging—of theory and fiction. With Haraway's *Staying with the Trouble*, for example, there are theoretical reflections about fiction and the importance of stories, but then there is also the writing of those stories themselves (often as part of a collective, as with 'The Camille Stories'). As both Haraway and Le Guin persuasively argue, it is important, here, that we also think about what stories we use to tell stories (and, for example, that we turn away from those Promethean meta-stories that have partly got us to where we are in terms of the various crises of the Anthropocene). To quote Haraway: 'It matters what thoughts think thoughts. It matters what knowledges know knowledges. It matters what relations relate relation. It matters what worlds world worlds. It matters what stories tell stories' (Haraway 2016: 35). With Haraway, there are also reflections within the stories she narrates about the importance of storytelling (for example, for the future communities Camille is part of). Finally, there is a turn in the other direction and the offering up of these stories and their avatars for use by others, a making-available of these elements and invented personae as resources, that is, a commoning (so, again, a collective storytelling is implied and called for). As Haraway puts it: 'The Camille stories are invitations to participate in a kind of genre fiction committed to strengthening ways to propose near futures, possible futures, and implausible but real nows' (Haraway 2016: 136). Theory-fiction seems to allow for these collective practices of imagining otherwise and, indeed, for these circuits of fiction and meta-fiction (or theoretical reflections on fiction) to take place. Or, once again, theory-fiction can be a place where the nesting and performance of different fictions is in play when this includes the travel and traversing between fictions.

Outside Perspectives and Critical Fabulations

Fiction—and Science Fiction most obviously—can then be concerned with a kind of performance of non-human perspectives (the writings of Octavia E. Butler would be a further key example here).[31] Or, put differently, fiction can offer an alternative optic on the world or even an optic on different worlds. When this is brought into relation with theory then what might be called this philosophical aspect of fiction is foregrounded or framed. Might it also be that theory-fiction works to offer an optic on a more radical 'outside'? Or, at least, gesture towards such perceptual possibilities, that is, towards passageways and exits from so-called reality? Perhaps theory-fiction can even give instructions, at least of a kind, on this mode of travel? This seems to be partly the case with Justin Barton's theory-fiction *Haunted Valleys* (2015), but also, more generally, characterises Barton's theoretical take on fiction in which literature is seen as a key resource for any excursion towards the outside or, indeed, for registering incursions from the outside (and in relation to this it is worth noting that Barton also collaborated with Mark Fisher). This is also a theme—or *concern*—of Reza Negarestani's writings, not least *Cyclonopedia*, which attends, in part, to how the outside might be lured in (I will return to this key work of theory-fiction below). Negarestani is another alumnus of Warwick University and connected to that Ccru scene I mentioned in the earlier sections of this essay.

   Barton's writings concern what he calls lucidity, a mode of being and awareness turned towards the planet and larger non-human world (so there are connections here with what I said above in relation to ecopoetics). His writings also highlight another aspect of theory-fiction—one that again moves it towards autotheory—simply that it can involve an imbrication of the personal with the theoretical (so there is an emphasis on 'situated knowledge' to use a phrase from Haraway [1991]). Here the blurring is less around theory and fiction and more around theory and a lived life (alongside any use of fiction within this set-up). Or, put differently, theory-fiction involves a blurring between different kinds of fiction; after all, we all inhabit our own fiction of the self, and this fact is certainly emphasised when a life is written.

A more personal register—or one in which the theoretical is related directly to lived life—is also present within those accounts of 'marked bodies' (as McKenzie Wark calls them [Wark 2020]) and/or the afterlives of slavery, as for example with Christina Sharpe's *In the Wake* (2016) and, more obliquely (at least in relation to the author's own life), Sadiya Hartman's *Wayward Lives, Beautiful Experiments* (2021). In both of the latter cases, the thematising of the self and/or individual experience in the writing is especially important (and appropriate) given that this kind of theory is about how bodies and lives have been impacted—or marked—by larger socio-political factors and traumas (in this case the trans-Atlantic slave trade). These kinds of writing—that involve fabulation and/or an auto-style—are then especially good at attending to the circuits and connecting lines between historical events and wider socio-political factors and an individual life. They might be understood as a form of minor literature in this sense, although in their attention to historical trauma and its continuing effects in the present, they also go well beyond Deleuze and Guattari's criteria. These kinds of text also have resonances with some of what I have said above about theory-fiction and time-looping (or the way in which writing can make different times present). For Hartman especially, fiction has a particular role to play in this creative and critical archival work and in the production of what she calls 'counter-narrative' (Hartman 2021: xvi). Critical fabulation—as method—also gestures forwards to some of my comments below in so far as it can involve the use of found photographs (as prompts) and then also the folding in—or fictioning—of other genres as well as a play with different styles and forms of presentation (as, for example, with the presentation of the 'Cast of Characters' at the beginning of *Wayward Lives, Beautiful Experiments* or the way in which that book moves between perspectives and subject positions/narrators). As Hartman puts it in 'A Note on Method': 'I employ a mode of close narration, a style which places the voice of the narrator and character in inseparable relation, so that the vision, language, and rhythms of the wayward shape and arrange the text' (Hartman 2021: xv-xvi). The method needs to be experimental and fabulatory insofar as a book like *Wayward Lives, Beautiful Experiments* sets out to explore those lives and ways of living that have been left out of or obscured by dominant history. Theory-fiction, if this method can be called as such, has an ethical and political urgency in these texts (or, put differently, writing here becomes part of a decolonial struggle). I will return to this—specifically in relation to the use of an auto style of writing—in my next essay).

Different Registers

As well as being a genre that explores other perspectives and agencies, theory-fiction might also be a name for theoretical work that mobilises other registers of representation as part of its method (besides the written). I have already mentioned this above (for example, in relation to Taussig's presentation of his drawings from his fieldwork notebooks), but to be more explicit here: it might, for example, involve drawings and diagrams as in Reza Negarestani's *Cyclonopedia* (2008). Negarestani's important work of theory-fiction looks back to the Ccru and, indeed, exemplifies their idea that diagrams might themselves be part of a hyperstitional practice.[32] In fact, more generally, diagrams can be thought of as a kind of theory-fiction insofar as they allow and partake of that combinatory function I mentioned above. Diagrams are a kind of imaging—or fictioning—of concepts in this sense. They also allow a more experimental and synthetic take on conceptual material (see a discussion along these lines in O'Sullivan 2016). A different take on this idea that theory-fiction can involve the use of different registers is the way it might turn to the comic-book or zine form, as for example, with Negarestani's collaboration with Keith Tilford and Robin Mackay on the theory-fiction comic *Chronosis* (2021).[33] This collaborative work looks back to various examples of comic books and graphic novels that deal with philosophical themes such as those by Alan Moore or Grant Morrison. Here theory-fiction utilises the particular combinatory effect of placing text and image together at the same time as referencing various precursors and more pulp antecedents. I will return to this area—of experiments in text and image, but also with form and presentation more generally—in my essay on art writing.

To switch the registers more radically, theory-fiction might also involve audio elements and especially voice (so sonic theory-fiction) as in Barton and Fisher's audio-dérive along the Suffolk coast, *On Vanishing Land* and, more recently, Robin Mackay's meditation on the town of Dunwich (also involving Fisher), *By the North Sea*. It might also involve images and sound (so audio-visual theory-fictions or what have also been called film-essays and docufictions) as in Victoria Halford and Steve Beard's mytho-poetic *Voodoo Science Park* or the fictioning of archives in some of the film-essays of the Otolith Group. Burrows and I have written extensively about these different forms of theory-fiction in our book on *Fictioning* (2019), so I won't repeat that material here except to point to the way in which theory-fiction can operate beyond the written word and, indeed, the book/essay form (and, once again, can involve the imbrication of the personal with the theoretical as well as the past/future with the present).[34]

Might we say, more generally, that theory-fiction utilises other modes—different forms and genres—but also different media that are not typically understood as being the remit of theory (so, again, theory-fiction as a kind of 'non-standard' theory)? Haraway also calls for this deployment of different media in her own writings ('*The story I tell here cries out for collaborative and divergent story-making practices, in narrative, audio and visual performances and texts in materialities from digital to sculptural to everything practicable*' [Haraway 2016: 143–144]), but to partly turn back to the Ccru—and to track a further genealogical trajectory—there are also the early performative theory-fictions from Nick Land (for example, at the *Virtual Futures* conferences at Warwick University in the 1990s).[35] These performance lectures (if they can be called as such) look back to a tradition of performance art but also gesture forwards to a group like Black Quantum Futurism (BQF) who also use performance as a part of their theory-fiction explorations of time travel. Here, it is also the way these other forms of presentation allow a break with standard modes and models that is important, not least—in relation to BQF—of a Western idea of linear time (see, for example, the discussion in Phillips 2018). In all these cases, fiction is used (as a resource) but also as a kind of method; or, put another way, the different components—audio, visual, theoretical—are used in such a manner that they bring or conjure a world. Theory-fiction has a performative dimension in this sense and can operate as a kind of summoning of different spaces and places and times and temporalities (when this also includes the performance of the retro-causality I mentioned above in relation to hyperstition).[36]

Formal Devices

To turn back to writing more specifically, on a formal level there seem to be two key characteristics to theory-fiction. Firstly, it is often more experimental than literature (or theory, for that matter), either in its overall presentation/format or in its style and syntax (which means it resonates with what has been called art writing). Secondly, it tends towards genre fiction (especially, as I have already gestured to above, Science Fiction), or, it might be said, avoids more typical narrative tropes and devices (and even more especially a certain kind of linearity that accompanies that mode). On the one hand, these two—experimentation and realism (at least of a kind)—are opposing tendencies. Perhaps, however, they are simply two poles—situated away from the more typical novel form—that theory-fiction oscillates between? Might it also be the case that theory-fiction involves a self-conscious play between these two categories of fiction? An example here, once again, is Negarestani's *Cyclonopedia* (2008) which, as I mentioned above, involves diagrams and other drawings and plays with style and presentation, but also deploys a Science Fiction (and Gothic) narrative in its account of a non-human agent—oil—and wider concepts and figures about our relationship (or non-relationship) with the outside. *Cyclonopedia*'s density (in content and style), its use of drawings and diagrams, its breadth of conceptual invention and the way in which it tacks between fiction and geography/geology/politics/history (but is also as if it has arrived from the future) makes it perhaps the key work of theory-fiction (at least, in terms of what I have come across). Once again, it seems to me that this book also started a whole genre of theory-fiction but also looks back to the style and methods of Deleuze and Guattari's 'Geology of Morals', for example.

Following these comments and to foreground something I have already mentioned above, theory-fiction, more simply, might be a name for those texts that perform their content in some form. Again, this has been implied in some of what I have already laid out above (and is certainly the case with texts like Deleuze and Guattari's *Anti-Oedipus*, for example, which is about connections and partial-subjectivities, and also plugs in to other connective 'machines'), but to make it explicit: theory-fiction can be understood as writing in which the style—syntax, presentation and so forth—and perhaps also the structure of a given text—emphasises or contributes directly to the conceptualisations and theoretical machinery. A good example here—that harks back to some of the cybernetic theory-fictions I mentioned above (and especially the theory-fictions of Plant, Land and the Ccru)—is Kodwo Eshun's sonic fiction, *More Brilliant than the Sun* (Eshun 1998). Eshun, who was associated with the Ccru, writes in a declarative and performative mode, with the invention of new terms, alongside cuts and breaks in the text and the insertion of quotes. The writing proceeds at a certain speed and with a kind of staccato rhythm. This book develops a particular idea of 'sonic fiction' (following, especially Sun Ra) but is also an example of sonic fiction. It reads like the music it writes about. In its turn to Sun Ra—and especially the idea of assembling 'counter mythologies' (Eshun 1998: 158)—it also foregrounds the idea of claiming a narrative that is in play with some other theory-fiction I mentioned above (for example, Hartman). In Eshun's book, this claiming of a narrative is also a claiming of the history of Black music.[37] Like Negarestani's *Cyclonopedia*, Eshun's book has also instigated a genre of sorts.[38] Another work in this vein is Stefano Harney and Fred Moten's *The Undercommons* (Harney and Moten 2013). Here, the style of writing contributes to the content and argument around 'Black Study' (or, again, the book performs this content). There is a kind of scene or feel to the writing, which is also what the writing is about. The text can be difficult to follow, with its loops and jumps, odd word choices and sentence structures and, indeed, abrupt switches between theoretical and more poetic modes (the latter following Moten's own poetic practices). *The Undercommons* frustrates a certain kind of reading and, indeed, calls to be performed somehow. This text also foregrounds collaboration and an idea of more collectively produced theory-fiction.[39] Once again, there is a sense of reclaiming a collective narrative here and, indeed, a calling forth of a community for whom this text is written.[40]

Performing Texts

To take all this a little further—and, again, make explicit something already implied in much of what I have written above—perhaps theory-fiction is writing that itself needs to be performed in some manner? I will address this area in more detail in relation to art writing in my third essay, but we might note here that there are all sorts of writing—instructions, protocols, spells and so forth—where this performative element is fore-grounded. A key precursor to this kind of theory-fiction is Georges Bataille. See, for example, the published collection of writings from the secret society *Acéphale* that involves various maps, lists, protocols and so forth (Bataille 2017). More generally, Bataille also utilises the first-person pronoun in his writing as a kind of performative device (so here it is not a confessional or authentic voice).[41] This is a further key characteristic of some theory-fiction that can involve this staging or performing of the 'I' (as, for example, also with the Steve Beard book I mentioned above), but it is even more in play with autofiction (that in many ways is defined by this staging) and art writing (that often also involves a more experimental staging of the self). I will return to this theme in the following two essays.

French Feminist theory would be a more literary example of this fore-grounding of the 'I' (and in this sense can be understood as a further pre-cursor to theory-fiction). In some of the texts associated with this scene there is a call for a new kind of writing—see as indicative Cixous (1981) and Irigaray (1985)—but also, crucially, an embodiment or pre-view of that writing in the call itself (so there is a hyperstition of sorts at play here).[42] Cixous also draws attention to the problem or knot that has been in play with some of the other theory-fiction texts I have already mentioned (such as Harney and Moten's): how to express a different mode of existence from within a more dominant one? Language must be made to speak otherwise or, to quote Cixous on what she calls a feminine writing practice, 'it does and will take place in areas other than those subordinated to philosophical-theoretical domination. It will be con-ceived of only by subjects who are breakers of automatisms, by peripheral figures that no authority can ever subjugate' (Cixous 1981: 253).

Another text that does this work is Monica Wittig's *Les Guérillières* (1971), which is about a community of lesbian women but also, as it were, from them and, indeed, paradoxically, one that calls them forth. There is an odd nesting of fiction in this work (that resonates with my comments above in relation to the Ccru) insofar as the women in the fictional community read the *feminaries* book, which might or might not be *Les Guérillières* (or part of that book). And this nesting moves in the other direction too, as when *Les Guérillières* is used as a kind of prompt to produce other work or, indeed, other communities (fictional or otherwise).[43] Once again, the fiction moves between different realities or even ontological layers. *Les Guérillières* also plays with different styles and registers, as in the listing of names in capitals (which read like incantations or spells) or the presentation of 'O' on different pages of the book (and the discussion of the significance of the letter). There are also the strong images and set-pieces and, indeed, sensuousness of the writing.[44] This work, although a fiction, seems to me to operate as a theory-fiction in these different ways but, especially in its nesting function or the way in which it inserts one fiction in another—and then also the way it has been utilised outside the fiction in other artists' practices, for example.

Staying with this nesting function, there are also those texts that involve a reading or folding of another's text within them. Or, indeed, the use of another's text as a kind of prompt for the writing. A recent example here is Alex Pauline Gumb's *Dub: Finding Ceremony* (2020) which partly nests the work of Sylvia Wynter within its pages. Another example— more on the fiction side of theory-fiction—is the Sellars book mentioned above where Ballard is the prompt. The writer David Berridge also sees this foregrounding of 'reading as practice' as characteristic of art writing, especially when the mechanics of reading or other kinds of interaction with a text are laid bare and made part of the writing (for example, when 'the reader-artist gives material form to their acts of reading, confidently altering or deleting the source text' [Berridge 2013: 10]), but it is also here in theory-fiction to some extent as when a text involves a kind of self-conscious commentary on (or an account of reading) another's text or when deploying a more performative mode in relation to another's text (as is the case with the Gumbs book mentioned above).

Sites of Production and Modes of Existence

Finally, theory-fiction is also related to its sites of production and what has become known as 'para-academia'. An implication here can be that it is less serious or, indeed, less academic, but, as I hope I have shown, it also means it has a different kind of traction on its readers and the worlds it is situated within. Theory-fiction is also often associated with publishers outside the usual university and other academic/scholarly presses or, indeed, larger fiction publishing houses (although this does seem to be changing).[45] Attending to these more socio-economic factors would be to shift the definitions of and propositions for theory-fiction from content and style to modes of production and, crucially, also of distribution. Indeed, it is because theory-fiction is from these other spaces and places that it can be involved in experimentation in both format and genre. A good example here is the publisher Urbanomic, which publishes works of philosophy and theory-fiction that would be unlikely to be published elsewhere (and, previous to this, also the Ccru pamphlets/zines).[46] But at the same time as this attention to print publishing, theory-fiction has also blossomed through websites (a recent example is 'Vast Abrupt') and blogs (a key precursor—and progenitor of a scene of sorts [the blog scene of the late nineties and early noughties]—being Mark Fisher's 'K-Punk'). Indeed, it is this—the proliferation of writing outside of at least some gatekeepers—that seems also to characterise theory-fiction (in fact, these are connected: ubiquitous digitisation has also brought about a renewed interest in self-publishing, artist's books and the like).

This focus on the spaces and places of production and dissemination and circulation and on the book form itself loops us back around to my comments made towards the beginning of this essay. Theory-fiction is not just situated between two different kinds of writing—and does not simply blur the border between them. Or rather, these traverses and crossings, as well as anything else, are a way of disabling certain boundaries and genres with their associated authorities and institutions. Ultimately, it is this promiscuous character of theory-fiction which means it is able to explore other perspectives and set-ups.

As I have implied in some of the above, it also seems to be the case that theory-fiction—like other kinds of hybrid writing—is a method of exploring other modes of existence. Ultimately, it seems to me that it can operate at the edge of the symbolic or in terms of what Raymond Williams once called those 'structures of feeling' that are pre-emergent (see the discussion in Williams 1977). How to write yourself when you are situated in a language and genre that are not yours? How to do philosophy when you are not—and do not want to be—a Philosopher? Other modes of existence need other modes of expression. This is certainly the case with the turn to autofiction/theory for trans writing, as I will explore in my next essay.[47] I will also return to this idea of writing expressing other modes of existence in my coda to 'On Art Writing' that looks at some specific case studies that might be said to move from art writing to theory-fiction.

As I mentioned above in relation to Harney and Moten and Wittig (and we also see in Haraway's collective storytelling and the writings of the Ccru), there is also the importance here of writing that is both from and for a collective. Indeed, this seems crucial to these 'new' genres of writing. They are from different agencies (away from the individual) but are also often future-oriented, calling forth other modes of existence from within this one. In fact, pushing this further, might we say that theory-fiction foregrounds the idea of writing as itself an agency—pitched against any single human originator—and, as such, might theory-fiction also be understood as the 'evil twin' of some examples of autowriting that attempt to hold on to the idea of the human as sole author and subject (or, at least, with theory-fiction there is a kind of fictioning of the later). Ultimately, then, theory-fiction is a kind of collective enunciation, or, to repeat perhaps the key point here, it is both from a scene and helps call that scene forth.

Coda: Scenes as Theory-Fiction

The above account of theory-fiction and my tentative attempt at some definitions and propositions arises from the different scenes I am familiar with and, more generally, my own situated perspective here in London and the UK in 2024—but also looking back to the 1990s which were a key time of intellectual formation for me. There are certainly other kinds of theory-fiction (or fiction theory, fictocritiscism and so forth) that have been left out of my account or, indeed, that I am unaware of. There are other narratives to be written (and no doubt are being written or have already been written), just as there are other scenes that are experimenting with writing that tacks between theory and fiction. Likewise, there are other histories and genealogies to these genres of writing that could be written. In terms of my particular perspective and in relationship to the Ccru (perhaps the key scene of theory-fictions for me), my attendance at two of the *Virtual Futures* conferences at Warwick University in 1995 and 1996 had a determining impact on my own academic trajectory and interest in theory-fiction (see also my comments in O'Sullivan 2014). In particular, it was the way in which at those conferences academic work was brought into encounter with more counter-cultural practices (especially rave culture). An example here is the way in which there were DJ decks set up in the main speaker's venue and, indeed, how the evening events were a crucial part of the whole set-up (or were seen as an integral part of the whole event). For myself, coming from an involvement in club and rave culture (in Leeds), this felt like a productive and exciting synthesis. There was also the way flyers and other textual and visual materials were circulating at *Virtual Futures*.[48] The whole scene felt very different to the usual academic set-up that I had become more used to or, put more strongly, here was an example of the integration of theory into lived life as well as the situating of the latter as an active site or medium of theoretical exploration.

Accompanying this—or as part of it—was also a more intense engagement with materials, whether practices or texts, and, once again, a kind of living out of them (or so it seemed to me back then). There was a certain affect or set of affects in play at those events that then triggered or prompted further work. What I saw and heard—and experienced—at those conferences was a different way of doing a certain kind of theoretical work, one that also involved an intensity and affective register (and the writings of Deleuze and Guattari were a crucial aspect of this).[49] Certainly the personal (at least of a kind) and the theoretical were also tightly enmeshed, albeit *Virtual Futures* also involved a turn away from the individual as sole agent in terms of cultural and theoretical production.

In relation to this, there was also the future orientation of the whole set up which felt like a kind of Science Fiction. *Virtual Futures* performed its content in this way. Would it be too much of a stretch to suggest that in this foregrounding of the affective—or again, a certain intensity—alongside this future orientation (as if the event were thrown back from a future), that *Virtual Futures* was itself a theory-fiction? Certainly, as I have suggested above (and will return in my essay 'On Art Writing'), a scene is often the generator of these new genres of writing. Or, a scene is needed to generate them, but these new genres can also themselves call forth different scenes (so, the retroactive feedback loop again).

Writing *Fictioning* with David Burrows and that other key scene of theory-fiction that I have discussed in this essay—around sympoiesis and inter-species relations—became crucial. Or that scene and how it was connected to feminist theory-fictions and, indeed, decolonial ones too. Certainly, encountering this latter material worked as a corrective to the more Promethean stories and cybernetic theory-fictions connected to the Ccru and those that came after. This kind of theory-fiction—I am thinking here especially of that which is concerned with the non-human—also connects to landscape and to the outside (so, once again, there are resonances here to ethnopoetics and ecopoetics). I have written more about this relationship of landscape, fiction and performance in a recent volume of essays that parallel this short book *From Magic and Myth-Work to Care and Repair* (O'Sullivan 2024). But in this context, it is worth remarking that there is also a sense that this other kind of theory-fiction— about our relationship to the non-human as well as our relation to one another—can also be involved in calling forth a scene or, indeed, more generally, new communities and collectives. And that here writing can be about—but also be a way of enacting or performing—the care and repair necessary for these coming communities, as well as for those communities that are already here and that we are already part of.

Notes

1. What follows is not the first attempt to track through and map out the genre/practice of theory-fiction (following the work of Mark Fisher especially). See, in particular, Gregory Marks' 'A Theory-Fiction Reading List'—that includes useful sub-divisions between 'theoretical titles which utilise fictional forms', 'fiction with theoretical content' and texts that 'occupy a space between these two, including the texts out of which "theory-fiction" emerged as a concept'—on his 'Wasted World' blog (https://thewastedworld.com/2018/11/03/a-theory-fiction-reading-list/) and the recent article on 'Science Fiction as Theory Fiction' by Javier Padilla (2022) that looks at many of the same texts as myself, but with a particular eye—as the essay title suggests—to the intersections and resonances between theory-fiction and Science Fiction.

2. In terms of Deleuze and Guattari, there is also *Anti-Oedipus* (1984) in which fiction is as much a resource as theory or philosophy—and in which the perspective of, for example, Daniel Paul Schreber (see 2000) is taken as seriously as (or more seriously than) Lacan (Schreber's account is a kind of auto-writing in which the life being recounted is undergoing a psychic break [and the auto-healing of that break]). Two other key precursors here (to the current scene of theory-fiction) are Artaud and especially his later writings (see Artaud 1995) and Jean-François Lyotard's *Libidinal Economy* (1993).

3. In fact, there is a sense that 'theory' already implies this different take on conceptual materials (so it is different from philosophy per se) or, at least, involves a different take on the realm of the application of concepts. See, for example, Mark Fisher's account of his interest in theory and, especially how he picked this up from music journalism ('My interest in theory was almost entirely inspired by writers like Ian Penman and Simon Reynolds, so there has always been an intense connection between theory and pop/film for me' [Fisher 2018a: 66]). See also Fisher's own body of theoretical writing that looks at fiction or uses it as a resource (for example, Fisher 2014 and 2016) or that involves a more direct take on—and, indeed, a coining of the term—theory-fiction (Fisher 2018b [thesis of 1999]). For another take on 'theory' in a similar sense, see Sylvère Lotringer and the Semiotext(e) project/publications, which for a certain generation (my own) more or less defined the genre of theory (and which also in its Native Agents series—initiated by Chris Kraus—published theoretically orientated fiction).

4. See as indicative Laruelle's essay 'Photo-Fiction, A Theoretical Installation' (Laruelle 2012a) and the discussion in O'Sullivan 2017c. Laruelle also has a more experimental and speculative side to his non-philosophy project with the actual writing of what might be called theory-fiction (see the texts gathered together at the end of Laruelle 2012b).

5. See also David Maroto's recent exploration of fictocriticism (specifically in relation to artistic research) (Maroto 2023). In relation to my own exploration of different genres of writing, Maroto suggests that, in fact, fictocriticism is best understood as not a genre but a practice (as we shall see Lauren Fournier makes the same claim in relation to autotheory): 'Fictocritical writing is not a style or a genre, in the sense that there is no set of conventions through which one can master it. It is an approach to writing that is eminently experimental and hybrid in nature' (Moroto 2023: 76). Maroto discusses a work—Katrina Palmer's *The Dark Object*—that I also look to in my essay on art writing and, more generally argues (as I do in this book) that it is the performative quality of fictocriticism that in part marks it out from other academic writing and art criticism.

6. Èdouard Glissant takes up this call to attend to minor literature in his own account of creolisation (see Glissant 2010). Interesting here—and in relation to what I will come to later in terms of theory-fiction utilising other registers of representation—is also the way Glissant includes a small drawing—even a kind of diagram—of the 'Middle Passage' on the first page of his book.

7. It is worth presenting the full passage from *Zeros and Ones* here (also to give a sense of Plant's style of writing):

> Fictions might be speculative and inspire particular developments, but they were not supposed to have such immediate effects. Like all varieties of cultural change, technological development was supposed to proceed step after step and one at a time. It was only logical, after all. But cyberspace changed all this. It suddenly seemed as if all the components and tendencies which were now feeding into this virtual zone had been made for it before it had even been named; as though all the ostensible reasons and motivations underlying their development had merely provided occasions for the emergence of a matrix which Gibson's novel was nudging into place; as though the present was being reeled into a future which had always been guiding the past, washing back over precedents completely unaware of its influence. (Plant 1997: 13)

8. In relation to this, see also McKenzie Wark's idea of 'low theory', another concept developed from the Situationists (and which is how Wark positions her own work): 'What has escaped the institutionalization of high theory is the possibility of *low theory*, of a critical thought indifferent to the institutional forms of the academy or the art world' (Wark 2015: 3). It seems to me that it is entirely possible to draw a trajectory from Wark's low theory here to her more recent writings on autotheory (Wark 2020), both being concerned with writing—and lived experiences—outside of the academy and other institutions (I will return to Wark's recent writings in 'On Autofiction and Autotheory').

9. To quote Plant at length again (this time quoting Foucault):

> Only when digital networks arranged themselves in threads and links did footnotes begin to walk all over what had once been the bodies of organized texts. Hypertext programs and the Net are webs of footnotes without central points, organizing principles, hierarchies. Such networks are unprecedented in terms of their scope, complexity, and the pragmatic possibilities of their use. And yet they are also—and have always been—immanent to all and every piece of written work. 'The frontiers of a book,' wrote Michel Foucault long before these modes of writing hypertext or retrieving data from the Net emerged, 'are never clear-cut: beyond the title, the first lines, and the last full stop, beyond its internal configuration and its autonomous form, it is caught up in a system of references to other books, other texts, other sentences: it is a node within network.' (Plant 1997: 10)

> See also Kenneth Goldsmith's account of *Uncreative Writing* (Goldsmith 2011) that attends to the way in which technology (and especially increased and accelerating reproducibility) has changed the status of writing (and creativity) and, more recently, Nathan Allen Jones's account of *Glitch Poetics* (Jones 2022), which names those forms of writing (and other practices) where digital technology—especially when it glitches or disrupts communication/information—brings about new modes of expression.

10. We made our argument there in relation to—and partly against—Quentin Meillassoux's idea of 'Extro-science Fiction', a genre within a genre that names those Science Fictions in which science, broadly understood, does not hold (to different degrees) (Meillassoux 2015). Our argument was that this schema might be pushed further or thought in

relation to those fictions that also take this logic into the syntax and style of writing itself—so, in this case, Science Fictions that break with straightforward narrative (cause-and-effect sequencing) and/or perform their content (as with *Cyberpositive*).

11. See, for example, Parisi's *Abstract Sex* (2004). I attend to Ireland's own writings—and theory-fictions—in a little more depth in an essay on 'Time Circuits and Loops' (O'Sullivan 2024).

12. And just as Haraway moves from the cyborg and technology to thinking about the Anthropocene, so too do another cyberfeminist collective—or theory-fiction assemblage—VNS Matrix who re-emerged after a long hiatus with their 'Hex for the Anthropocene'. In relation to the formats and forms of theory-fiction, see also their *Hex* fanzine (VNS Matrix 2015). In relation to a continuation of the technologically mediated cyberfeminist project (in terms of writing), see the *Xenofeminist Manifesto* by the collective Laboria Cuboniks (2015).

13. See also Land's more recent theory-fictions (for example, Land 2015) that also foreground the importance of the genre of horror (and especially Lovecraft) in this particular genre of theory-fiction (what might be called a conjuring of the Outside). For a recent theory-fiction that follows Land's account of geotrauma, see Moynihan (2019). See also the writings of Masciandaro (2014) and Thacker (2011) that might be said to be part of this 'horror-theory-fiction' genre (or, at least, are writings *on* the latter). Masciandaro writes on *Cyclonopedia*, Gnosticism and the Outside. Thacker writes on Black Metal, demonology and occult philosophy. For both, H. P. Lovecraft is a key resource (as it is for Deleuze and Guattari).

14. See also Burroughs's comments about the cut-up operating as this kind of feedback loop from the future back into the present:

> I would say that my most interesting experience with the earlier techniques was the realization that when you make cut-ups you do not get simply random juxtapositions of words, that they do mean something, and often these meanings refer to some future event. (Burroughs 2005: 28)

15. In relation to these temporal circuits and to fictions that mix together different times, see also the genre—if it can be called as such—of neomedievalism and, especially the books by the Confraternity of Neoflagellants (2013, 2021) that play with style and syntax (and presentation more generally) in offering up their singular future-past visions (see also the

discussion about the first of these two books in Burrows and O'Sullivan 2019: 110–113). The second of these books—*Pan-Pan*—might also be described as art writing (albeit of a very wonky kind).

16. As Fisher remarks in the essay and blog post 'Why K-Punk?': 'The whole pulp theory/theory-fiction thing was/is a way of doing theory through not "on", pop cultural forms' (Fisher 2018a: 31). There is a fourth important pre-cursor to mention here, albeit from a different US scene, Steven Shaviro and especially his *Doom Patrols*, subtitled *A Theoretical Fiction about Postmodernism* (1997), which contains chapters on Burroughs and Acker (amongst others). More generally, Shaviro's own writing trajectory is characterised by working across and between theory (and philosophy) and fiction (and especially Science Fiction).

17. This also resonates with Isabelle Stengers's account of animism and magic and the idea of fictions having real effects and thus being, to that extent, real (see Stengers 2012 and my discussion in 'Avatars, Egregores and the Fiction of the Self' in *From Magic and Myth-Work to Care and Repair* [O'Sullivan 2024]). See also Félix Guattari's account of 'fabulous Images'—especially as found in Jean Genet's writings—that track across from literature to life (Guattari 2013).

18. To quote the Ccru:

> for practitioners of hyperstition, differentiating between 'degrees of realization' is crucial. The hyperstitional process of entities 'making themselves real' is precisely a passage, a transformation, in which potentials—already active virtualities—realize themselves. Writing operates not as a passive representation but as an active agent of transformation and a gateway through which entities can emerge. '[B]y writing a universe, the writer makes such a universe possible'. (Ccru [and quoting Burroughs] 2017: 36)

19. To quote the Ccru again:

> Diagrams, maps, sets of abstract relations, tactical gambits, are as real in a fiction about a fiction about a fiction as they are encountered raw, but subjecting such semiotic contraband to multiple embeddings allows a traffic in materials for decoding dominant reality that would otherwise be proscribed. Rather than acting as transcendental screens, blocking out contact between itself and the world, the fiction acts as a Chinese box—a container for sorcerous interventions in the world. The frame is both used (for concealment) and broken (the fictions potentiate changes in reality). (Ccru 2017: 38)

20. See, for example, the discussion of Russell Hoban's *Riddley Walker* in my essay 'Fictioning a Pilgrimage (or Fieldwork on the Fiction of the Self)' (O'Sullivan 2012).

21. In the text 'The Electronic Revolution', Burroughs also refers to L. Ron Hubbard's take on language/engrams as a kind of magical practice:

> Mr. Hubbard has charted his version of what he calls the reactive mind. This is roughly similar to Freud's id, a sort of built-in self defeating mechanism. As set forth by Mr. Hubbard this consists of a number of quite ordinary phrases. He claims that reading these phrases, or hearing them spoken, can cause illness, and gives this as his reason for not publishing this material. Is he perhaps saying that these are magic words? Spells, in fact? (Burroughs 2005: 26)

> Certainly, Burroughs saw the cut-up as likewise a magical—or occult—technology (see the discussion in Burrows and O'Sullivan 2019: 35–43). Also relevant here is the way in which Burroughs writes about 'Playback' as a kind of magical practice or how the insertion of one fiction within another can change that fiction (so, here, representation is used—or doubled—in order to produce a desired effect). To quote Burroughs: 'make recordings and take pictures of some location you wish to discomode or destroy, now play recordings back and take more pictures, will result in accidents, fires, removals' (Burroughs 2005: 10).

22. See especially Burroughs's cut-up trilogy and Ballard's *The Atrocity Exhibition* (1993 [1970]).

23. For a tracking through of theory-fiction's relation to Science Fiction, see the Padilla article mentioned in my first note to this essay.

24. See also Alice Bucknall's 'New Mystics' project that utilises AI language prompts in relation to a collaboration with various artists currently involved in practices at the intersection of magic and technology (http://www.newmystics.xyz/about/). As with K Allado-McDowell, the results of these collaborations with the text-generating AI can be a little clunky, although my sense is that this is just to do with teething problems with these new AI systems (there is, however, also a danger that these 'new' kinds of writing become caught in a certain genre, especially when they follow what might be called 'New Age' prompts).

25. See also the discussion about other perspectives—and the Science Fiction devices that might enable these—in Burrows and O'Sullivan 2022.

26. As Deleuze remarks—in relation to this invention of concepts—at the very beginning of his major work and key philosophical statement *Difference and Repetition*: 'A book of philosophy should be in part a very particular species of detective novel, in part a kind of science fiction' (Deleuze 1994: 6). See also Steven Shaviro's ongoing project of reading Science Fiction philosophically (Shaviro 2015, 2021).

27. See the texts gathered together in *#Accelerate: The Accelerationist Reader* (Mackay and Avanessian 2014).

28. See especially the essay on 'The Carrier Bag Theory of Fiction' (Le Guin 1989) in which Le Guin writes against those Promethean stories that invariably involve a male hero figure and his weapons, turning instead towards other kinds of framings and meta-narratives:

> If, however, one avoids the linear, progressive, Time's-(killing)-arrow mode of the Techno-Heroic, and redefines technology and science as primarily cultural carrier bag rather than weapon of domination, one pleasant side effect is that science fiction can be seen as a far less rigid, narrow field, not necessarily Promethean or apocalyptic at all, and in fact less a mythological genre than a realistic one. (Le Guin 1989: 170)

29. I look at a recent example of this kind of writing and genre in my coda to the essay 'On Art Writing'.

30. See also various collective theory-fictions or world-building projects that involve new technologies and/or collaborations with non-human species (as called for by Haraway and others), such as etic lab (https://eticlab.co.uk/)

31. See the discussion of *Adult Rites* in Burrows and O'Sullivan 2022. As regards Octavia E. Butler, there is also the way her fiction, in this case the novel *Kindred*, is used by Denise Ferreira da Silva as a kind of prompt in her own theoretical work and analysis of coloniality and race (see Ferreira da Silva 2022).

32. See the Ccru quote in note 19.

33. In terms of zines and theory-fiction (and, indeed, the connection of the latter to counter-cultural scenes), see also Laura Oldfield Ford's *Savage Messiah* project (Oldfield Ford 2011).

34. See Burrows and O'Sullivan 2019: 138–140 (*On Vanishing Land*) and 229–232 (on the film-essays of the Otolith Group). See O'Sullivan 2018 for a discussion of *Voodoo Science Park*.

35. See the account given by Robin Mackay in 'Nick Land: An Experiment in Inhumanism' (Mackay 2012).

36. See also the Ccru's numogram and the *Syzygy* collaboration with 0[rphan] d[rift>] archived here: https://www.orphandriftarchive.com/becoming-cyberpositive/syzygy/syzygy2/

37. To quote Eshun on this reclaiming (and to get a sense of his own style and sonic fiction):

> To listen to Ra is to be dragged into another sonar system, an omniverse of overlapping sonar systems which abduct you from Trad audio reality. By becoming alien himself, Ra turns you alien. Afro < > American history is white mythology [...] Reject history and mythology. Assemble countermythologies. (Eshun 1998: 158)

38. See, for example, Goodman (2010) and Audint (2011) and, for a survey of this field opened up by Eshun, Schulze (2020).

39. In relation to collaboratively produced theory-fictions, see also the work of The Occulture (David Cecchetto, Marc Couroux, Ted Hiebert and Eldritch Priest), for example, *Ludic Dreaming* (2017), which deploys fiction (and dreams) as part of its theoretical explorations.

40. An indicative example (also of the style of this book):

> But this is to say that there are flights of fantasy in the hold of the ship. The ordinary fugue and fugitive run on the language lab, black phonography's brutally experimental venue. Paraontological totality is in the making. Present and unmade in presence, blackness is an instrument in the making. (Harney and Moten 2013: 94)

41. See Nick Land's *Thirst for Annihilation* (Land 1992), which draws attention to this performative device in Bataille's writings (more generally, Land's book is intent on interrogating the idea of the self [so might be understood as a kind of anti- or non-autowriting]). In relation to Bataille—and an auto and performative style of writing—see also the recent volume of collected writing on Acèphale and 'autobiographical philosophy' (Connole and Shipley: 2021).

42. In relation to theory-fiction and the field opened up by French feminist writing, there is also the writing and art practice of Bracha Lichtenberg Ettinger and Elizabeth Samsonow, both of whom invent figures and devices and thus might be understood as working between theory and

fiction or even as developing different theory-fictions (see, for example, Ettinger 2006 and Samsonow 2010).

43. See, for example, Mai-Thu Perret's 'The Crystal Land' and Beatriz Santiago Muñoz's 'Song, Strategy, Sign' but also Plant's turn to Wittig in her own work of theory-fiction (Plant 1997).

44. An indicative quote:

> Somewhere there is a siren. Her green body is covered with scales. Her face is bare. The undersides of her arms are a rosy colour. Sometimes she begins to sing. The women say that of her song nothing is to be heard but a continuous O. That is why this song evokes for them, like everything that recalls the O, the zero or the circle, the vulval ring. (Wittig 1971: 14)

45. See, for example, the 'Unidentified Fictional Objects' imprint of Goldsmiths Press.

46. See especially the recent 'Switch' imprint of Urbanomic.

47. The key text here is Paul Preciado's *Testo Junkie* (2013). See the discussion of this—and other works of autofiction/theory—in 'On Autofiction and Autotheory'.

48. For an example of how the academic here dovetailed with the counter-cultural, see the essays and play with presentation of Matt Fuller's edited collection *Unnatural* (1994) (which includes the 'Cyberpositive' essay by Land and Plant mentioned above). There is another account to be written of how counter-cultural writing can involve a theory-fiction register (and this would link back to—or form a constellation with—various Lettrist and Situationist texts such as those by Asger Jorn [see, for example, Jorn 1994]). Once again, there is a writing here that is from and for a scene.

49. I also experienced something similar at the 'Bataille Now' conference held upstairs in the Packhorse pub in Leeds in 1995. The venue played a key part here, but it was also the way some of the speakers approached Bataille's writings and indeed, the way the conference talks bled into the ongoing conversations and other activities that went on well into the night (in fact, into the next morning).

References

Artaud, Antonin (1995), *Watchfiends and Rack Screams: Works from the Final Period of Antonin Artaud*, ed. and trans. C. Eshleman and B. Bador, Boston: Exact Change.

Audint (S. Goodman, T. Heys and E. Ikoniadou) (2011), *Unsound: Undead*, Falmouth: Urbanomic.

Barton, Justin (2015), *Hidden Valleys: Haunted by the Future*, Winchester: Zero Books.

Bataille, Georges (2017), *The Sacred Conspiracy: The Internal Papers of the Secret Society of Acéphale and Lectures to the College of Sociology*, eds. M. Galletti and A. Brotchie, trans. N. Lehrer, J. Harman and M. Barash, London: Atlas.

Beard, Steve (2019), *Six Concepts for the End of the World*, London: Goldsmiths Press.

Berridge, David (2013), *Man Aarg!: Poetry, Essay, Art Practice*, London: NØ Demand at X Marks the Bøkship.

Bratton, Benjamin H. (2015), *Dispute Plan to Prevent Future Luxury Constitution*, Berlin: Sternberg.

Burroughs, William (2005), *The Electronic Revolution*, New York: ubuclassics. Available at: www.ubu.com/historical/burroughs/electronic_revolution.pdf (accessed 29 January 2017).

Burrows, David and S. O'Sullivan (2019), *Fictioning: The Myth-Functions of Contemporary Art and Philosophy*, Edinburgh: Edinburgh University Press.

—— (2022), 'Science Fiction Devices', *New Perspectives on Academic Writing*, London: Bloomsbury, pp. 39–52.

Cixous, Hélène (1981), 'The Laugh of the Medusa', trans. K. Cohen and P. Cohen, *Signs*, 1.4: 875–93 (reprinted in *New French Feminisms: An Anthology*, E. Marks and I. de Courtivron (eds.), Hemel Hempstead: Harvester Wheatsheaf, pp. 245–64.

The Confraternity of Neoflagellants (N. Hogg and N. Mulholland) (2013), *thN Lng folk 2go: Investigating Future Premoderns*, New York: Punctum Books.

—— (2021), *Pan-Pan*, New York: Punctum Books.

Connole, Edia and G. J. Shipley (2021), *Acéphale and Autobiographical Philosophy in the Twenty First Century*, London: Schism Press.

Cybernetic culture research unit (Ccru) (n.d.), 'Hyperstition'. Available at: https://web.archive.org/web/20030204195934/http://ccru.net/syzygy.htm (accessed 5 September 2021).

——— (2017), 'Lemurian Time War', *CCRU Writings 1997-2003*, Falmouth/ Shanghai: Urbanomic/Time Spiral Press, pp. 33–52.

Deleuze, Gilles (1994), *Difference and Repetition*, trans. P. Patton, New York: Columbia University Press.

Deleuze, Gilles and F. Guattari (1984), *Anti-Oedipus: Capitalism and Schizophrenia*, trans. R. Hurley, M. Seem and H. R. Lane, London: Athlone Press.

——— (1986), *Kafka: Towards a Minor Literature*, trans. D. Polan, Minneapolis: University of Minnesota Press.

——— (1988), *A Thousand Plateaus: Capitalism and Schizophrenia*, trans. B. Massumi, London: Athlone Press.

——— (1994), *What is Philosophy?*, trans. H. Tomlinson and G. Burchell, London: Verso.

Eshun, Kodwo (1998), *More Brilliant Than the Sun: Adventures in Sonic Fiction*, London: Quartet.

Ettinger, Bracha L. (2006), 'Matrixial Trans-subjectivity', *Theory, Culture & Society*, 23: 2–3: 218–22.

Ferreira da Silva, Denise, (2022), *Unpayable Debt*, London: Sternberg.

Fisher, Mark (2014), *Ghosts of my Life: Writings on Depression, Hauntology and Lost Futures*, London: Zero Books.

——— (2016), *The Weird and the Eerie*, London: Repeater.

——— (2018a), *K-Punk: The Uncollected and Unpublished Writings of Mark Fisher (2004–2016)*, ed. D. Ambrose, London: Repeater.

——— (2018b), *Flatline Constructs: Gothic Materialism and Cybernetic Theory-Fiction*, New York: Exmilitary Collective.

Fuller, Matt (1994), *Unnatural: Techno-Theory for a Contaminated Culture*, London: Underground.

Glissant, Édouard (2010), *Poetics of Relation*, trans. B. Wing, Ann Arbor: University of Michigan Press.

Goldsmith, Kenneth (2011), *Uncreative Writing: Managing Language in the Digital Age*, New York: Columbia University Press.

Goodman, Steve (2010), *Sonic Warfare: Sound, Affect, and the Ecology of Fear*, Cambridge, MA: MIT Press.

Guattari, Félix (2013), 'Genet Regained', *Schizoanalytic Cartographies*, trans. A. Goffey, London: Bloomsbury, pp. 215–30.

Gumb, Alexis Pauline (2020), *Dub Finding Ceremony*, Durham: Duke University Press.

Haraway, Donna (1991), 'Cyborg Manifesto: Science, Technology and Socialist Feminism in the Late Twentieth Century', *Simians, Cyborgs and Women: The Reinvention of Nature*, London: Free Association Books, pp. 149–82.

——— (2016), *Staying with the Trouble: Making Kin in the Chthulucene*, Durham, NC: Duke University Press.

Harney, Stefano and F. Moten (2013), *The Undercommons: Fugitive Planning and Black Study*, New York: Autonomedia.

Hartman, Saidiya (2021), *Wayward Lives, Beautiful Experiments: Intimate Histories of Riotous Black Girls, Troublesome Women and Queer Radicals*, London: Serpent's Tail.

Irigaray, Luce (1985), *The Sex Which is Not One*, trans. C. Porter and C. Burke, New York: Columbia University Press.

Jorn, Asger (1994), *Open Creation and Its Enemies*, trans. F. Tompsett, London: Unpopular Books.

Jones, Nathan Allen (2022), *Glitch Poetics*, London: Open Humanities Press.

K Allado-McDowell (2020), *Pharmako AI*, Newcastle-on-Tyne: Ignato.

Laboria Cuboniks (2015), 'Xenofeminist Manifesto'. Available at: http://www.laboriacuboniks.net (accessed 11 July 2022).

Land, Nick (1992), *The Thirst for Annihilation: Georges Bataille and Virulent Nihilism*, London: Routledge.

——— (2011), *Fanged Noumena: Collected Writings 1987–2007*, ed. R. Mackay and R. Brassier. Falmouth: Urbanomic.

——— (2015), *Phyl-Undhu: Abstract Horror, Exterminator*, Shanghai: Time Spiral Press.

Land, Nick and S. Plant (1994), 'Cyberpositive', *Unnatural: Techno-Theory for a Contaminated Culture*, ed. M. Fuller, London: Underground.

Laruellle, François (2012a), 'Photo-Fiction, A Theoretical Installation', *Photo-Fiction: A Non-Standard Aesthetics*, trans. D. S. Burk, Minneapolis: Univocal, pp. 11–24.

——— (2012b), *From Decision to Heresy: Experiments in Non-Standard Thought*, trans. R. Mackay, Falmouth/New York: Urbanomic/Sequence Press.

Le Guin, Ursula K. (1989), 'The Carrier Bag Theory of Fiction', *Dancing at the Edge of Time: Thoughts on Worlds, Women and Places*, New York: Grove Press, pp. 165–70.

Lyotard, Jean-François (1993), *Libidinal Economy*, trans. I. Hamilton Grant, London: Athlone.

Mackay, Robin (2012), 'Nick Land: An Experiment in Inhumanism'. Available at: https://readthis.wtf/writing/nick-land-an-experiment-in-inhumanism/ (accessed 26 February 2024).

2 On Theory-Fiction   43

Mackay, Robin and A. Avanessian (eds) (2014), *#Accelerate: The Accelerationist Reader*, Falmouth and Berlin: Urbanomic/Sequence.

Masciandaro, Nicola (2014), *Sufficient Unto the Day: Sermones Contra Solicitudinem*, London: Schism Press.

Meillassoux Quentin (2015), *Science Fiction and Extro-Science Fiction*, trans. A. Edlebi, Minneapolis: Univocal.

Maroto, David (2023), 'Valid Fictional Contributions to Non-Fictional Debates: Fictocritical Writing in Artistic Research', *Acta Academiae Artium Vilnensis*, 109: 65–83. Available at: https://doi.org/10.37522/aaav.109.2023.160 (accessed 26 August 2023).

Moynihan, Thomas (2019), *Spinal Catastrophism: A Secret History*, Falmouth: Urbanomic.

Negarestani, Reza (2008), *Cyclonopedia: Complicity with Anonymous Materials*, Melbourne: re.press.

Negarestani, Reza, K. Tilford and R. Mackay (2021), *Chronosis*, Falmouth: Urbanomic.

The Occulture (David Cecchetto, Marc Couroux, Ted Hiebert, Eldritch Priest) (2017), *Ludic Dreaming: How to Listen Away from Contemporary Technoculture*, London: Bloomsbury.

Oldfield Ford, Laura (2011), *Savage Messiah*, London: Verso.

0[rphan] d[rift>] (2012 [1996]), *Cyberpositive*, London: Cabinet Gallery.

O'Sullivan, Simon (2006), *Art Encounters Deleuze and Guattari: Thought Beyond Representation*, Basingstoke: Palgrave.

——— (2012), *On the Production of Subjectivity: Five Diagrams of the Finite-Infinite Relation*, Basingstoke: Palgrave.

——— (2014), 'The Missing Subject of Accelerationism', *Mute*. Available at: www.metamute.org/editorial/articles/missing-subject-accelerationism (accessed 7 November 2023).

——— (2016), 'On the Diagram (and a Practice of Diagrammatics)', *Situational Diagram*, eds. K. Schneider and B. Yasar, New York: Dominique Lèvy, pp. 13–25.

——— (2017a), 'Memories of a Deleuzian: To Think is Always to Follow the Witches Flight', *A Thousand Plateaus and Philosophy*, eds. H. Somers-Hall, J. Bell and J. Williams, Edinburgh: Edinburgh University Press, 2017, pp. 172–89.

——— (2017b), 'Accelerationism, Hyperstition and Myth-Science', *Cyclops*, 2: 11–44.

———— (2017c), 'Non-Philosophy and Fiction as Method', *Fiction as Method*, eds. T. Reeves-Evison and J. K Shaw, Berlin: Sternberg, pp. 273–318.

———— (2018), 'Fictioning the Landscape', *Journal of Aesthetics and Phenomenology*, 5.1: 53–65.

———— (2024), *From Magic and Myth-Work to Care and Repair*, London: Goldsmiths Press.

Padillia, Javier (2022), 'Science Fiction as Theory-Fiction', *Modernism/Modernity*, 6.3. Available at: https://modernismmodernity.org/forums/posts/padilla-science-fiction-theory-fiction (accessed 3 September 2022).

Parisi, Luciana (2004), *Abstract Sex: Philosophy, Bio-Technology and the Mutations of Desire*, London: Continuum.

Phillips, Rasheedah (2018), 'Placing Time, Timing Space: Dismantling the Master's Map and Clock', *The Funambulist*, 18. Available at: https://www.blackquantumfuturism.com/articles-guest-writing (accessed 6 May 2022).

Plant, Sadie (1992), *The Most Radical Gesture: The Situationist International in a Postmodern Age*, London: Routledge.

———— (1997), *Zeros and Ones: Digital Women and the New Technoculture*, London: Fourth Estate.

Preciado, Paul B. (2013), *Testo Junkie: Sex, Drugs, and Biopolitics in the Pharmacopornographic Era*, trans. B. Benderson, New York: The Feminist Press.

Samsonow, Elizabeth (2010), 'Anti-Electra: Totemism and Schizogamy', trans. V. Faessel and S. Zepke, *Deleuze and Contemporary Art*, eds. S. Zepke and S. O'Sullivan, Edinburgh: Edinburgh University Press, pp. 246–65.

Savransky, Martin (2021), *Around the Day in Eighty Worlds: Politics of the Pluriverse*, Durham, NC: Duke University Press.

Scott, David (2000), 'The Re-enchantment of Humanism: An Interview with Sylvia Wynter', *Small Axe*, 8: 119–207.

Schulze, Holge (2020), *Sonic Fictions*, London: Bloomsbury.

Schreber, Daniel Paul (2000), *Memoirs of My Nervous Illness*, New York: New York Review of Books Classics.

Sellars, Simon (2018), *Applied Ballardianism: Memoir from a Parallel Universe*, Falmouth: Urbanomic.

Sharpe, Christina (2016), *In the Wake: On Blackness and Being*, Durham and London: Duke University Press.

Shaviro, Steven (1997), *Doom Patrols: A Theoretical Fiction about Postmodernism*, London: Serpent's Tail.

———— (2015), *Discognition*, London: Repeater Books.

——— (2021) *Extreme Fabulations: Science Fictions of Life*, London: Goldsmiths Press.

Stengers, Isabelle (2012), 'Reclaiming Animism', *e-flux*. Available at: http://www.e-flux.com/journal/36/61245/reclaiming-animism   (accessed   5 September 2021).

Taussig, Michael (2010), 'The Corn Wolf: Writing Apotropaic Texts', *Critical Inquiry*, 37.1: 26–33.

——— (2011), *I Swear I Saw This*, Chicago: Chicago University Press.

Thacker, Eugene (2011), *In the Dust of this Planet: Horror of Philosophy Vol. 1*, Alresford: Zero Books.

Tsing, Anna Lowenhaupt (2015), *The Mushroom at End of the World: On the Possibility of Life in Capitalist Ruins*, Princeton: Princeton University Press.

Viveiros de Castro, Eduardo (2014), *Cannibal Metaphysics*, trans. P. Skafish, Minneapolis: Univocal.

VNS Matrix (2015), *Hex* fanzine, no. 2.

Wagner, Roy (2010), *Coyote Anthropology*, Lincoln and London: University of Nebraska Press.

Wark, McKenzie (2015), *The Beach Beneath the Street: The Everyday Life and Glorious Times of the Situationist International*, London: Verso.

——— (2020), 'Girls Like Us', *The White Review*. Available at: https://www.thewhitereview.org/feature/girls-like-us/ (accessed 30 November 2023).

Williams, Raymond (1977), *Marxism and Literature*, Oxford: Oxford University Press.

Wittig, Monique (1971), *Les Guérillières*, trans. D. Le Vay, London: Peter Owen.

3

On Autofiction and Autotheory

Abstract There is a thin line between autofiction and autotheory, just as there is between biography—or memoir—and autofiction. But a tentative definition is that autofiction is writing in which the author is a character in some form and autotheory is writing that is self-consciously situated between the self (however that is defined) and theory (in whatever way that term is understood). This short essay explores these two forms of writing, especially as they relate to what I call the 'fiction of the self'. As with the previous essay, different examples are brought in to build a theoretical argument. The seven thematic sections of this essay are as follows: (1) Autowriting and the Self. Here, I introduce these new genres of autowriting (especially in relation to McKenzie Wark's and Laurent Fournier's definitions). (2) Marked Bodies and Situated Theory. In which I survey some of the field and attend to the marginal history of some of this writing. (3) Genre and Desire. In which I look to how the self is brought into writing or how the self is already written. (4) Cut-Ups and Fold-Ins. In which I explore some more experimental methods of autowriting. (5) Afterlives, Autoethnographies and Nervous Systems. Where I briefly consider an auto style of writing more generally. (6) Fictioning the Self. In which I make the claim I mentioned above about autofiction staging the fiction of the self in different ways. (7) Mirrors and Prisms. In which I explore autowriting as a kind of optical device. The essay ends with a brief coda in which I write about my own experience teaching an MA seminar on autofiction and autotheory.

© The Author(s), under exclusive license to Springer Nature Switzerland AG 2024   **47**
S. O'Sullivan, *On Theory-Fiction and Other Genres*,
https://doi.org/10.1007/978-3-031-65072-7_3

Keywords Autofiction • Autotheory • Autoethnography • Cut-Up • Situated Theory • Fictioning

Autowriting and the Self

There is a thin line between autofiction and autotheory, just as there is between biography—or memoir—and autofiction.[1] But a tentative definition is that autofiction is writing in which the author is a character in some form—as, for example, in one of the first contemporary examples of this genre, Chris Kraus's *I Love Dick* (Kraus 2006); and autotheory is writing that is self-consciously situated between the self (however that it defined) and theory (in whatever way that term is understood)—so autotheory looks back to works like Gillian Rose's *Loves Work* for example (Rose 1995).[2] Autofiction then necessarily involves some kind of reflection on the self as fiction (even if that remains implicit rather than explicit) or even an exploration of the self as constructed through fiction.[3] Autotheory involves a reflection on the imbrication of the self with theory (even if that is manifested mostly through style and presentation) or even, perhaps, a theory of the self as fiction (again, whether explicit or implicit).[4] As Mackenzie Wark suggests in her essay 'Girls Like Us', autotheory might also be understood to involve a different take on theory in general, as no longer abstracted or extracted from a life (hence the resonances with theory-fiction) (see Wark 2020a). This is theory as part of lived experience or even as a survival strategy of sorts. Wark's essay is especially concerned with trans writing and, indeed, the various issues involved in writing about another's pain or staking a claim on it. For Wark, there is a class issue here or, more simply, a question of money and of who has the time and the space to write their own (or another's) narrative. As she remarks, 'writing about pain requires painless days' (Wark 2020a). Finally, there is the suggestion from Lauren Fournier that autotheory might be thought of less as a genre (which autofiction might still be) and more as a practice (see Fournier 2021).[5] As Fournier also remarks early on in her book on *Autotheory* (in relation to Maggie Nelson's distinguishing of 'life-writing'—a key written form of autotheory—from memoir): 'life-writing is distinguished by its ontology as a practice—something active that one does in the present—rather than a genre, which is more static and fixed, shaped by pre-existing categories and generic expectations' (Fournier 2021: 14). For Fournier, it is this that links autotheory to art practice and, in her own mapping out of a genealogy, specifically to feminist art practices (see Fournier 2021: 1–69).[6] Autotheory might be understood as just the latest name for a particular intersectional feminist method—one that for Fournier is 'transmedial'—of foregrounding the self in theoretical work.[7] It is an aesthetic choice, but, crucially, also involves a political imperative. In relation to some of my comments about theory-fiction in the previous chapter, we might say autotheory—like that other kind of writing—pitches itself against master discourses.

Marked Bodies and Situated Theory

For Wark, autotheory is also a form of 'situated' theory, especially when it is written by and about what she calls 'marked' bodies (and her own essays on autowriting, in their attention to their own conditions of production—Wark's life and motivations/desires around writing—are an example of the autotheory she writes about). To quote Wark: 'autofiction is the literature where the marked self—marks itself. The writer marked by gender, sexuality, race, is supposedly cut off from universality' (Wark 2020a: n. p.).[8] In passing, and in relation to this idea of marked bodies, we should also note a key 'sub-genre' of autofiction/ theory (although not one I go into any detail about in this essay): 'Sick Woman Theory' or what is also known as 'crip theory'. This writing concerns bodies marked by illness (and, in some cases, marked by less visible illness). Key texts here are Joanna Hedva's essay on 'Sick Woman Theory' (2015), Dodie Bellamy's essay (in the book of the same title) 'When the Sick Rule the World' (2015) and, more recently, Alice Hattick's *Ill Feelings* (2023). The latter especially foregrounds an idea of self-care (and writing) as survival.

Autofiction, for Wark, also involves written narratives of those lives left out of the grand stories (of Modernism).[9] For Wark, it is a form of fiction pitched against the bourgeois novel, when this is understood as an essentially proprietorial form of cultural production (not least in terms of the self).[10] In all these ways, for Wark, autofiction and autotheory are both marginal and urgent. In her essay on autofiction, 'Girls Like Us' (2020a) —and a more recent one on 'Critical (Auto) Theory' (2023)— Wark offers up a genealogy of autowriting, leading, specifically, to trans writing (and in the latter essay, to her own works of autofiction).[11] Elsewhere—in a conversation with Fournier—it is suggested that other genealogies would be possible (see, for example, my brief comment above about crip theory) (see Fournier and Wark 2020). From Fournier's perspective, and as I also mentioned above, this involves a turn to various art practices, especially feminist ones, in which the self is foregrounded or where there is an emphasis that 'the personal is political'. Fournier also suggests that theory in general—insofar as it is necessarily written from a certain perspective—might be understood as always already a kind of autotheory. Certainly, that theory in which an author's style and subjective perspective is foregrounded might be understood as leaning this way.[12]

There is an interesting contretemps here which Wark and Fournier discuss in a podcast (see Fournier and Wark 2020). On the one hand, writing is the expression of a subject and thus the argument might be made, again as Fournier suggests, that all writing is necessarily a kind of autowriting (to collapse autofiction and autotheory together for the moment) whether such writing directly concerns the self or not. And yet, on the other hand, all writing is simply text and, as such—as Wark points out—it is impossible to locate any one, single author. Writing dismantles the idea of a singular authorial intention, as Roland Barthes announced all those years ago.[13] In many ways Barthes can be seen as a key precursor of autotheory (and autofiction) and especially of those examples that foreground their textual character (or foreground the textual character of the self more generally). I have in mind here not just Barthes's influential essay on 'The Death of the Author', but also works like *A Lover's Discourse* (1979) (from which Maggie Nelson took the title of her *The Argonauts*) and *S/Z* (1975), a sustained meditation on narrative codes—and of the role of the reader in relation to any interpretation—in Balzac's short story 'Sarasine'. This would also be to track and map out a longer and larger genealogy of autotheory in relation to critical theory. Wark's essay on 'Critical (Auto) Theory' also suggests this kind of genealogy of autowriting in its own bringing in of Barthes and others (and, indeed, literary history and theory more generally).

Following Barthes then, an author is, in this sense, a kind of imaginary projection of us, the reader. Where does this leave autofiction and autotheory? If an author is indeed produced through reading, then might we say that some of these 'new' kinds of autowriting are also the result of a certain kind of reading (or even the birth of a 'new' kind of reader?).[14] As far as this goes, autofiction, for example, would be a regressive action of bringing the author back in (or, again, of us as readers desiring and thus producing a singular author). This would also be the case with that autotheory that attempts a straightforward folding together of its subject/author and theory (as in theoretical writing that leans towards the biographical).

It is in this respect that the turn to autowriting in some cases is a turn away from the poststructuralist critique of the author. But this does not mean it is simply a conservative or reactionary move. Reintroducing the author in many of these cases is also to affirm the importance of race and gender (for example)—Wark's 'marked' bodies—within these subject positions. Fournier's book also demonstrates how an auto method of writing and practice has political implications (and has a history—again, as for example in feminist art practice—prior to being labelled autotheory). Autowriting foregrounds this situatedness of its author, but also—in a kind of recursive circuit—it can throw the reader back on themselves or prompt them to reflect on their own perspectives (and, crucially, sometimes their own privileges). Here, autowriting is both an example of self-positioning (by the author), and about positionality in general (in relation to theoretical knowledge and our personal investments in the latter). Or, put differently, autowriting is both from a specific author *and* does something to the perspective of its readers (or, following Barthes, it implicates its readers in its method). I'll return to this double function below.

Genre and Desire

Another approach to these definitions and propositions might also be to simply understand autofiction and autotheory as both involving a certain style of writing and thus as a genre (despite Fournier's comments). Reading a selection of contemporary autofiction there are certainly recognisable tropes and constructions in play that might constitute something we could call (a) genre. As Wark herself acknowledges (Fournier and Wark 2020), she borrows stylistic elements from Maggie Nelson's *The Argonauts* (2016)—which is a kind of contemporary ur-autofiction—in writing her own autofiction *Reverse Cowgirl* (2020b). In relation to autotheory, Nelson's text is especially interesting for the way it brings in its theoretical references as side notes alongside the confessional and at times intense narrative.[15] Indeed, it is the way in which it brings in theory, always related to the experiences of Nelson, that marked it out as particularly original when first published (albeit not without some more general precursors). Invariably, one gets a situation of texts that break with existing protocols—they try out something new—and then there are others that follow (in the parallel realm of theory-fiction—as I mentioned in the previous essay—Reza Negarestani's *Cyclonopedia* [2008] springs to mind as also the generator of a genre). This is not necessarily to denigrate those works that come after. Although it is often the case that the original is markedly better, sometimes the further takes on it—the repetitions—increase the power of the genre or push it further somehow. At any rate, it might well be that autowriting—again, to collapse both autofiction and autowriting together—is a practice (as Fournier suggests) or a set of tactics (as Wark has more recently claimed [Wark 2023])—but that it is also a genre in this sense of deploying a certain style and form. Again, this is especially the case when it is read or seen from an outside perspective, as it were.

To put this differently, autotheory and autofiction might be a practice in terms of writing (what else could they be), but in terms of reading they can be seen as a genre. The other interesting cases here are those writings that work from outside a given genre (including the genres of autowriting and autotheory), or which in some way do something to it (so again a repetition, but with difference). And then also those works that perhaps traverse these autowriting genres and other genres too (working diagonally, so to speak)—works that, as Wark remarks, 'lie askew' (Wark 2023: n. p.).[16] A good example here is *Psycho Nymph Exile* by Porpentine Heartscape, which is autowriting but also Science Fiction (2016). In its experimentation with form and presentation—including its presentation across media platforms (as well as a book)—it also gestures towards art writing. *Psycho Nymph Exile* partakes of, traverses, and then also does something to all these genres. But it is also different to all these genres and very much its own thing.

To move away from questions of genre and style for a moment and turn to the motivations and so forth for these new forms of autowriting: there certainly seems to be a will to attend to one's own history in the writing or to foreground an exploration of the self. In particular, there is often an attention to how desire circulates in a given life (this is especially the case with autofiction).[17] How it manifests within, but also problematises, a given narrative or, more generally, how a life narrative is characterised by its relation to desire (as, for example, with Maggie Nelson's *The Argonauts*, mentioned above, or, more recently, Mattilda Bernstein Sycamore's *The Freezer Door* [2020] that also involves a play with style, in this case a narration [of the self] through fragments). More particularly, there is attention to how a lived life connects to (or is determined by) larger circuits of desire and other, wider socio-economic contexts as, for example, with Paul Preciado's 'political experiment' and key trans autofiction/autotheory *Testo Junkie* (2013) (so an example of a minor literature in this sense—to briefly turn back to some of the comments I made in the previous essay—albeit, once again, going beyond any strict Deleuze/Guattari definition). Even more so than Nelson's book, it is this text by Preciado that announced a different way of writing theory in relation to the self and of connecting the latter to a larger context more generally.

Despite my comments about Preciado, there is, I think, a danger that some of this autowriting can result in the foregrounding of atomised individuality. Here, autowriting would be a symptom of a general narcissistic condition, part of our contemporary 'selfie culture' (autofiction, in particular, understood as a—rarefied—subset of celebrity culture, albeit often presented as non-celebrity writing).[18] As Wark suggests however—and as I mentioned above—it is also (for some) a way of narrating a life that has otherwise been obscured or of making visible a particular lived situation. As I gestured towards at the beginning of this essay, might there also be a sense in which autofiction especially is less the affirmation of an individual life—or not only that—and more an enquiry into the fiction—or fictions—of the self? An exploration of the parameters and logics of that fiction and then—why not?—a writing out of other possibilities (this is the fiction side).[19]

Certainly, even just to write oneself as a character—or as a number of characters—in a text is to get some perspective on that self (as Patrick Keiller suggests in his docufiction *London* [a cousin to autofiction, as the essay-film is a cousin to theory-fiction] this is a facet of Romanticism).[20] As well as a genre then, autowriting is a device that can foreground a different perspective on, and thus a different relation to, the self in this sense.[21]

Cut-Ups and Fold-Ins

Might this be at least one reason that trans writing so often uses an auto style/practice (that is, besides Wark's crucial point about narrating the lives of situated and marked bodies)? In many ways, trans experience is already a writing of the self—certainly, at least in many cases, it is a claiming of gender identity away from external determinants (again, see Preciado's *Testo Junkie* [2013]).[22] Pushing this further—and thinking, for example, of Genesis P. Orridge's pandogyne project—is the trans experience itself a form of cut-up when this names a cutting into and re-writing of a given script (as well as sometimes a more literal operation)? As a non-trans writer, there is a limit to my understanding here and I am also wary of making generalisations, but there does seem to be a 'tradition' in autowriting, following Preciado, of narrating the transition journey, as for example (and in a UK context) with Juliet Jacques' *Trans: A Memoir* (2019) (albeit this text does not play with form). It is useful here to turn back to Wark's own schema or topology of different kinds of trans literature (that she lays out in the essay 'Girls Like Us') and from which perspective some of these accounts of the trans journey repeat or utilise more mainstream or bourgeois tropes or reinforce a certain fiction of the self or even narrate the 'uncovering' of a more authentic self (as opposed to, for example, the more radical project of [de]constructing a self with someone like P-Orridge). On the other hand, sometimes a more straightforward register of realism is important, for example in clearly communicating (and, again, simply making visible) a specific life story.

In relation to this there is also that autowriting that involves a folding—or nesting—within itself of other life stories, other fictions of other selves. This seems to be especially the case with an author like Kathy Acker—who already uses plagiarism and pastiche as part of her method—and the various autofictions and autotheory written about and around her. See, for example, Chris Kraus's *After Kathy Acker* (2017), Olivia Laing's *Crudo* (2018) and (more autotheory) Wark's *Philosophy for Spiders* (2021).[23] Something like this nesting function is also in play with Alexis Pauline Gumbs's autotheory *Dub: Finding Ceremony* (2020a) which, as mentioned in my previous essay, involves a reading of Sylvia Wynter's work or, we might say, the use of Wynter's writings as a kind of prompt for further reflections and autowriting. There is a performative element at work here in the way in which this text addresses its reader (in other writings by Gumbs this can also involve sets of instructions to be followed [Gumbs 2020b]). It is interesting that this kind of work involves a kind of claiming of another's text—not from that perspective and position that Wark criticises as bourgeois writers staking claims on the pain of marked bodies (again, see Wark 2020a), but rather as a kind of 'writing-with' or alongside another author (albeit, without their consent). Or, put differently, this can be a kind of 'fan' writing with all that implies (an enthusiasm, an affective resonance, and so forth).[24] Another example of this folding in of another's text—and also another example of trans autotheory—is Andrea Long Chu's account of their reading of Valerie Solanas (in their book *Females*): a situated account of their reading and then a writing with or alongside Solanas (Long Chu 2019). Long Chu's text also concerns the interesting idea of 'gender as genre' and thus further accentuates the connections between autowriting (or other trans-genre/hybrid writing) and other modes of (gendered) existence. And then there is also, once again, Preciado's book that, in part, is prompted by (and about their relationship with) the writer Guillaume Dunstan.

Afterlives, Autoethnographies and Nervous Systems

The strategies used in some authotheory of absorbing and being absorbed by the texts of precursors, forbears and even antagonists—we might say, a particular relationship to the archive more generally—is also there in

Saidiya Hartman's ficto-historical work, for example, *Wayward Lives, Beautiful Experiments* (2021a) that I discussed briefly in the previous essay. And then there is also Hartman's more obviously auto writing, *Lose Your Mother* (2021b) that recounts her journey to and within Ghana—following the slave routes—and her enquiry into the afterlife of slavery. This using of the personal as a way in to thinking larger historical issues around trauma is also in play in Christina Sharpe's *In the Wake* (2016), which turns to an auto register so as to develop its arguments and frame its case studies (what Sharpe calls 'wake work').[25] I mentioned both of these writers in the last chapter but would highlight here how the weaving in of the personal with the political (or simply the moving between these different registers) gives this material more traction in and on our world. After all, the afterlife of slavery is not an abstract idea but is being lived and continues to mark bodies today (including the bodies of these writers).[26] As such, this register of autowriting (and, alongside that, other experiments in foregrounding the authorial voice [as well as furter experiments with style and presentation]) can, it seems to me, increase the impact of this kind of important work. Indeed, there is a sense that more typical academic writing (that is distanced, objective and so forth) and those knowledge economies it plugs into or is part of is also an aspect of the problem here (insofar as it is institutionally determined, involving exclusions and obscurations as well as other value systems, sometimes more implicit than explicit). An autowriting style or method in the texts mentioned above is part of the anti-colonial struggle in this sense when this is understood as a struggle that is also about foregrounding those modes of existence and voices that have been obscured or denigrated or (mis)represented by others.

There are other kinds of writing where an auto register also seems appropriate, if not crucial. An example is autoethnography, which I also briefly mentioned in the previous essay, for example with Anna Lowenhaupt Tsing's important work *The Mushroom at End of the World* (2015). The use of first-person accounts helps to foreground the way in which our ecological crisis impacts on actual lived lives. The focus on specific, local details—searching for a mushroom, for example—also allows a more embodied understanding of larger ecological and socio-economic issues. Again, the personal and the particular are used as a method to explore more global circuits and contexts. Or, to say the same differently, the various crises of the Anthropocene demand a different kind of writing that is appropriate for and adequate to 'living in the ruins' (so, not distanced and objective but subjective, changing perspective, curious and collaborative and so forth) on condition that this localism *also* finds a way to comprehend (and theorise) the full planetary scale. This writing can also provide other narratives for its readers or help 'address the imaginative challenge of living without those handrails, which once made us think we knew, collectively, where we were going' (Tsing 2015: 2). There is a connection here with what my comments in the previous essay about needing other kinds of stories besides the ones that have brought us to the present crisis and, following Donna Haraway and Ursula K. Le Guin, of especially attending to what stories we use to tell stories. Indeed, an auto style of writing might be understood as one of these meta-stories or framing devices that has an increasing importance in our contemporary world insofar as it can foreground the lived experience of different individuals and communities (especially, once again, of those that have not hitherto been written or heard).

Another example here is the writing—and the writing on writing—of the anthropologist Michael Taussig. In the last chapter, I mentioned Taussig's idea of a 'Nervous System' writing that pitches itself against 'agribusiness' writing (which he suggests is especially prevalent in the Academy). Agribusiness writing, for Taussig, can also be complicit in violence and extraction (it follows a colonial logic). Once again, at stake here is the question of 'What kind of story can cut across and deflect those violence-stories, this being every bit as much a question of art and ritual as it is of social science' (Taussig 2010: 32). As I also mentioned in the previous essay, Nervous System writing attends to the various slippages between ontological levels and to the performative character of writing more generally (or it is attentive to what writing *does* rather than what it explains). This involves 'the blurring of fiction and non-fiction, beginning with the recognition and appraisal that this distinction is itself fictional and necessary' (Taussig 2010: 33). Nervous System writing is then a form of experimental—and magical—field work.[27] Auto-ethnography, like autotheory more generally, also implicates its author in this work (after all, they are just one further fiction or ontological layer). Or, put differently, autoethnography involves a shift in perspective and even, perhaps, a looking back at the self from an elsewhere (that is, alongside any other content).[28]

Fictioning the Self

Does reading these different kinds of autowriting also allow a shift of perspective to be performed in some manner? Certainly, besides offering information about a particular situated life—or life situation—reading autowriting can allow a different relationship to the self to occur. It is as if reading a fiction which experiments in and around the reality/fiction border—or, in this case, puts the reality (of a given life) into the fiction—allows another point of view to be opened up. Gilles Deleuze writes about something similar in *Cinema 2: The Time Image,* where he outlines the importance of intercessors, real historical figures that can appear within certain fictions, in this case, films (see Deleuze 1989: 222). For Deleuze, these figures operate as a kind of bridge, giving a fiction a stronger traction in and on reality (hence their importance, especially for the political functioning of film). But we might also add that they do something to the viewer's (or reader's) own position (situated as the latter is in a certain reality). A kind of doubling of perspective can be produced by these films—and texts more generally—that play with fiction and reality in this way.[29] This can also work, more simply, when other fragments of the real world (or of a lived reality)—various details, for example—are included within a fiction (or even, relating to some of what I say above, in relation to various nesting and foldings—the inclusion of other fictions within a fiction). Certainly, the fictioning of reality within a text (if I can put it like that)—in a film, for example—works to increase the believability of the latter, but also, as a kind of side effect, it can foreground the fictional character of any 'external' reality that the reader/viewer is themselves situated in (when this also includes the self that is reading the text or watching the film).

This also works the other way around. Introducing fiction into so-called reality does something to that reality. As I suggested in my previous essay, fiction can have a transformative effect in and on reality in this sense (this is what might be called its magical effect). Autofiction, I think, is no different in this respect. It is a fiction that is put out into the world, which then, like other kinds of fiction, throws its context (in this case, the self) into doubt—or at least loosens things up a little—especially when it encounters a particular kind of reader. This is the case even if your life experiences are not 'trans' in the same way as some of the authors I have discussed in this essay. There are resonances and strategies to learn, as well as recursive circuits in play when we read these autowritings.

Autofiction—like fiction more generally (I am thinking especially of the novel form here, particularly when this involves a first-person perspective)—is like a strange hole in reality in this sense (the reality as experienced by a reader—the world they move in and through), and also a kind of lens and a mirror. A lens onto those other lives and worlds that the fiction concerns (this lens might also operate as a prism in terms of the dispersal of perspectives); a mirror in relation to the reader and their particular world (even if the latter is very different to the life being read about).[30] In terms of any lens, this might be relatively transparent, so that we are less aware there is a mediating device, or clouded with condensation on its surface—to use an image and metaphor from Félix Guattari (Guattari 1989: 219)—which means we see the other life-world and, at the same time, are aware of the glass through which we see it (which is partly how the mirroring function operates). Autofiction, and to a lesser extent autotheory, is then not only a genre and a practice but also a strange and multifaceted optical device in this sense, one that also self-consciously foregrounds its status as a made thing.

Mirrors *and* Prisms

A concluding word of warning to this short essay and something perhaps to bear in mind with all the essays collected in this book: seeing autofiction—and autowriting more generally—in terms of the self that is doing the reading can mean that these texts are co-opted. Or, put differently, the proprietorial function of bourgeois literature is transposed from the author (who, as Wark remarks, often writes about—and thus claims— these marked bodies) to the reader (who 'relates' these fictions to their own life). It is essential that these texts are not just seen as mirrors but as lenses and sometimes prisms too. To repeat the point above, they are optical devices that offer a view onto another life or into a diversity of other lives (or even work more simply so that these other lives are no longer invisible). This is also the case with those texts that are more ethnographic or ecopoetic in character and that offer, we might say, a wider and even more diverse/dispersed perspective onto other forms of nonhuman life. But without the mirroring function, without bringing a reader's own self into the frame, then these autowritings can remain simply curious objects—separate and distinct from the life in which they are found—that have no effect on the reader beyond curiosity or even voyeurism. Indeed, in the worst cases, this would be to render the lives being written about as simply interesting exceptions. Ultimately, then, it is this kind of double function of autowriting that seems important: that it necessarily comes from somewhere else—another life besides our own—and offers an optic onto that other life (or, indeed, other lives); but that it also frames and helps question the fiction of the self—the particular perspectives, attitudes and values (including often the privileges)—that is there doing the reading.

Coda: Autowriting and Community

In an MA seminar on autotheory and autowriting (part of a larger course 'On Theory-Fiction and Other Genres'), we read extracts from Fournier's book on *Autotheory* alongside Wark's essay 'Girls Like Us'. We also looked at extracts from Nelson's *The Argonauts* and Preciado's *Testo Junkie* alongside an extract from Alice Hattrick's *Ill Feelings* (2023). In the seminar discussion, it was especially the way in which these texts—particularly the latter three—involved disclosure and the foregrounding of vulnerability that meant they had traction on our own lives. It was this sense of vulnerability—and honesty—in and with this writing that appealed (as one of the participants of the seminar remarked, they made her feel more human). This had also been the case with some previous sessions on that particular course when we had looked at some of the texts I have already mentioned in my previous essay (especially in relation to the undercommons/Black Study and living in the ruins/staying with the trouble), but here the sense of vulnerability had more of an impact. It was the way in which these texts foregrounded the subjective experiences of their authors—and thus showed us what was at stake in their writing—that gave them this traction. It was partly reading these texts—this was the last seminar of the course—that helped the students cohere as a group. Some of these writings are for (and from) a particular community, whether that's the trans or the ill, but they also have this wider valency. Although autowriting is tethered to an individuated sense of self, paradoxically, these texts also help form or call forth a community—as demonstrated by this brief example of reading together.

Connected to this was also the style these texts are written in. There was a directness to all of them which nevertheless is never polemical. One of the participants in the seminar remarked of the Preciado that there was a sense of things just being said as they are without any attempt to 'hold the reader's hand'. But, again, this did not mean the texts were not generous. Indeed, it was something about the lack of compromise, that they were just what they were, that appealed and gave them this force. There was a sense that each of the texts was their own thing or even constituted their own genre as such. I will return this idea in the next essay of my book.

Related to this was also the fact that these texts were made things and foregrounded this fact in their structure, style or presentation. They were not autobiographies but autofictions. Or, put differently, the details of a life had been selected, and certain aspects foregrounded, specifically, in each case, in relation to various theoretical resources (so to repeat a key point I have already made above, there was certainly an imbrication of the personal and political just as there was a sense, especially with the Preciado, in which the personal was used as a way in to writing about 'larger' concerns). It was this, their status as representations, albeit ones more tethered to a particular life, that once again meant they had this attraction and valency beyond any authorial intention. It was as if they were a device, at once simple and complex, that could be used or, at least, had a function beyond the strictly literary, not least as a prompt for other work and other enquiries (they certainly operated as such for that seminar).

As with some of the texts I mentioned in the previous essay—and, again, this is a key theme of my own essays—there was then a performative aspect to this new genre of autowriting, in terms of what it can do and what the different texts within the genre can call forth. This is not to claim them or to remove them from their context and the lives being written about—indeed, their work as devices was to do with the way they embody a singular perspective and were tethered to a particular space and time. But it is to say that the texts seemed to have a function beyond being only this. They were able to travel. We might even say that their singular nature, to say it again, meant they were able to do the other kind of mirroring work I mentioned above. Once again, it seems to me that it is this double functioning—these texts operating as both mirrors *and* prisms—that, partly at least, defines them as autofictions and works of autotheory.

Notes

1. As with other essays in this book, my account of autofiction and autotheory draws on my own familiarity with just a selection of this field of writing, which is to say where the latter dovetails with contemporary art practice and associated fields of writing (so, for example, not the discipline of English literature). In fact, what follows draws particularly on the work of McKenzie Wark and Laurent Fournier, each of whom have come up with important definitions and propositions for autowriting (and, in Wark's case, key examples of it).

2. In relation to autotheory and its precursors, see also Jane Gallop's *Anecdotal Theory* (Gallop 2002), which foregrounds the feminist trajectory in and of this kind of writing. For a further example of contemporary autotheory—and turning away from feminist or indeed trans writing—see also Justin Barton's *Hidden Valleys* (2015) that I discussed briefly in the previous chapter (and also the discussion of that book in Burrows and O'Sullivan 2019: 139–140).

3. Or, as McKenzie Wark puts in a recent article on autowriting (her own and those she recognises as precursors):

   I think of autofiction as writing in which a character with the same name or attributes as the author appears, but where that character is not attempting to write the truth of the self, in the manner of memoir or autobiography. Selfhood itself is a fiction, and the writing is an account of how the fiction of a self is produced. (Wark 2023: n. p.)

In relation to this, see also Audre Lourde's *Zami: A New Spelling of My Name* (1982) and the idea/genre of 'biomythography', understood as the weaving together of myth, history and biography.

4. An interesting case study here is Terry Atkinson's *The AGMOAS is now a Corporate Audit* (2017) which as well as being an account of the artist's own history (an auto-history?) is also an account—and critique—of the still dominant 'avant-garde mode of artistic subjectivity' (as the acronym of the title announces). So, this text is an example of autowriting but also a critique of autowriting (insofar as the latter can sometimes be tethered to the AGMOAS).

5. Wark's recent article on 'Critical (Auto) Theory' offers up a further take on the difference between autofiction and autotheory—that they are to do with affects and concepts, respectively. This essay also offers up a more general take on autowriting as a set of tactics (rather than a genre):

I think of autotheory as not too different from autofiction. Both are interested in the perceptual. Autofiction is more interested in the affective dimensions of what's perceived; autotheory more the conceptual. It's more interesting to think of autofiction/autotheory as tactics rather than genres, and as a continuity of tactics. I'll call it the 'auto-textual': These practices made this self. (Wark 2023: n. p.)

6. In relation to autotheory and artistic practice, see also the special issue of *Arts* on 'Autotheory in Contemporary Visual Arts Practice'. The editor's 'Introduction', as well as drawing out a further genealogy, also points towards various limits and problems associated with the term autotheory (and with the practices it names), not least in relation to 'institutional power dynamics' and, indeed, whose autotheory is being written and read. To quote the editors (who quote Charlie Markbreiter): 'Autotheory does not automatically provide the level playing field that Fournier assumes, because "not everyone's interiority is received with the same candour"' (Baxter and Auburn 2023: 3). For another recent gathering of essays on—and examples of—autotheory, also in relation to themes such as precarity and non-human life, see the special issue of the *Journal of Writing in Creative Practice* on 'Ways of Writing in Art and Design II' (Sames 2023). The two-part special issue of this journal—edited by

Lucy A. Sames—arose from a research network based at the University of the West of England in Bristol, which, once again, foregrounds the importance of scenes in the generation of new genres of writing (and the role of writing—and editing—in the constitution of scenes).

7. More generally, Fournier's genealogy and various definitions of autotheory moves from philosophical precursors and avant-garde feminist art to practices by 'women, Indigenous artists, Black artists, POC artists, LGBTQQ2S+ artists, and poor and working-class artists' (Fournier 2021: 68). My own consideration of autotheory in this essay is restricted to writing (which is something Fournier also considers—for example, in the sustained reading of Nelson's *The Argonauts* and the references throughout to Kraus's *I Love Dick*—albeit these are thought through in the larger context of art practice).

8. Wark would seem to have Donna Haraway's essay on 'Situated Knowledges' in mind here and 'the gaze that mythically inscribes all the marked bodies, that makes the un-marked category claim the power to see and not be seen, to represent while escaping representation. This gaze signifies the unmarked positions of Man and White…' (Haraway 1988: 581).

9. To quote Wark on autofiction: 'It's for writers who never could quite place themselves in the big stories of their era, and perhaps that's why it has emerged from the margins in this time which has lost confidence in any grand narratives' (Wark 2020a: n. d.).

10. It is also for this reason that autofiction can involve a play with style and syntax and other formal devices. Wark addresses this in her essay 'Girls Like Us', laying out a schema of progressive experimentation, a move away from typical realism (although she is also keen to point out the importance of work—including her own—that situates itself away from any avant-garde traditions and tropes, especially in relation to what she calls 'low theory') (Wark 2020a). Autotheory might also be said to be a form of low theory insofar as it can involve blogs, fanzines and so forth that are written and distributed away from any centres or often even any margins of more mainstream literary cultures.

11. Wark also notes a near cousin of autofiction in the 'New Narrative' scene in the US. Interesting here—and this relates to Wark's own argument about trans writing—is that this form of writing is both from and for a collective. There is an apparent contradiction between the individual (the 'auto') and the community, but one that is generated by and generative of the actual writing: 'Its writers are in each other's books, as are

people who didn't get to write books, or who didn't even get to live. There's generative tension between the avarice of authorship and the ambience of a collectively made literary space, one that includes non-writers' (Wark 2020a: n. p.). I will return to this question of the auto and community in a brief coda to this essay.

12. As Fournier also suggests, a further genealogical line might also be made to French feminism, especially with writers like Luce Irigaray and Hélène Cixous who call for a 'new' kind of writing that attends to women's bodies and desire and, in this sense, tracks across the personal and political (or makes the personal political). To quote Cixous from 'The Laugh of the Medusa' specifically on this point: 'In woman, personal history blends together with the history of all women, as well as national and world history' (Cixous 1981: 252).

13. A process that has only increased—or, at least, been further fore-grounded—with the event of the digital. This attitude towards writing is exemplified within 'conceptual writing' (or post-internet writing). To quote Amy Ireland, who is herself quoting Brian M. Reed:

> Reed cites the increasing automation of writing processes currently deployed under the banner of conceptual writing, with their recon-figuration of the author as nothing more significant than 'just another content provider' carrying out repetitive, alienating tasks (transcrip-tion, copying, OCR, plagiarism, coding) that are 'as dreary as data entry'—and deliberately so. (Ireland 2017: 10)

> At the same time as this (or as part of this move towards author as 'content provider'), we see the foregrounding of the author and the self within social media (see my next note).

14. A new kind of reader who is caught in self-reinforcing circuits of repre-sentation and recognition, which is to say a reader at least partly deter-mined by the logics of social media (the latter being both a kind of autowriting [focused as it is on the representation of the self], as well as an anti-autowriting [insofar as there are pre-set forms and logics, or, more generally, that self is reduced to a restricted set of images]).

15. Like Paul Preciado's *Testo Junkie* (2013), Nelson's *The Argonauts* involves the description of sexually explicit scenes from the outset, something that also then determines, at least to some extent, a certain sub-genre of autowriting.

16. To quote Wark more fully on this point:

> I've always had a yen for books that lie askew. That play with genre as form, that tweak a reader's expectations. Books that, when you open them, open also towards uncategorized desires. Similarly with scholarly books: I like the ones that don't squat neatly in a field, that evade the keywords assigned to them, that refuse the private property system of owners and their claims to stake out the knowable. (Wark 2023: n. p.)

17. See also my essay 'Fiction as Desiring Work' in *From Magic and Myth-Work to Care and Repair* (O'Sullivan 2024: 23–32).

18. Although see also Matt Colquhoun's *Narcissus in Bloom* that makes the argument that the selfie might be indexed to the desire for and will to self-transformation (Colquhoun 2023).

19. As Preciado says at the beginning of *Testo Junkie*:

> This book is not a memoir. This book is a testosterone based, voluntary intoxication protocol, which concerns the body and affects of BP. A body-essay. Fiction, actually. If things must be pushed to the extreme, this is a somatopolitical fiction, a theory of the self, or self-theory. (Preciado 2013: 11)

20. In relation to this see the discussion of Keiller in Burrows and O'Sullivan 2019: 134–135. See also the way William Burroughs writes himself as a character into his writings (as 'Old Bull Lee') and more generally fictionalises real-life people and events (Burroughs 2008: 31).

21. In the book I wrote at the same time as this one—*From Magic and Myth-work to Care and Repair* (2024)—I attend further to this idea that fiction can offer a view back on the self and, indeed, the way in which a writing practice can be involved in a practice of repair of the self. In that book, it was especially Lacan's idea of the sinthome—a new knot that can retie the Real, Symbolic and Imaginary—that was in play (Lacan's case study is Joyce and, as such, we might say that Joyce's *Portrait of the Artist as a Young Man* is a further key precursor to autofiction).

22. In relation to trans as a refusal of binaries (and thus an affirmation of another mode of gender/exuality [or a proliferation of modes]), see also Preciado's more recent *Can the Monster Speak?* (2021), a transcript of a 'speech given by a trans man by a non-binary body before the École de la Cause Freudienne in France' (to quote the book's subtitle).

23. Wark also had a more direct relationship with Acker—but, again, one mediated by writing. See the letters published in Acker and Wark 2015. See also Linda Stupart's *Virus* (2016) for another kind of autotheory/ writing (a fictionalised autowriting?)—or 'art writing'—that also looks back to Acker (I will return to Stupart's book in my next essay).

24. In relation to this, see Catherine Grant and Kate Random Love's anthology of writings around *Fandom as Methodology* (2019). As they say at the very beginning of their 'Introduction' (comments that also relate to art writing):

> we take fandom seriously, particularly as a practice that can bring to light affective attachments, resistant reworkings *and* an acceptance of operating within a consumer culture that tries to instrumentalise fannishness … fandom is also a way to think of the ways in which artists engage with their subject matter that goes beyond the creative and critical, and combines scholarly attention with identification and desire. (Grant and Love 2019: 1-2).

See also Holly Pester's article 'Archive Fan-Fiction' (2017) that similarly argues 'for a discursive archive method that puts subject desire and embodied politics into a position of agency' (2017: 127) and her book *Go to Reception and Ask for Sara in Red Felt Tip* (2015) which is, at least in part, a poetic and idiosyncratic take on the archive (or a fictioning it) and further shows the blurred boundaries between art writing and autofiction/theory (Pester's book was the result of a residency at the Women's Art Library at Goldsmiths). Pester's writing on—and practice of—fabulation in relation to archive work resonates with Saidiya Hartman's method of critical fabulation that I briefly discuss below.

25. To quote Sharpe:

> If … we think the metaphor of the wake in the entirety of its meanings (the keeping watch with the dead, the path of a ship, a consequence of something, in the line of flight and/or sight, awakening, and consciousness) and we join the wake with work in order that we might continue to imagine new ways to live in the wake of slavery, in slavery's afterlives, to survive (and more) the afterlife of property. In short, I mean wake work to be a mode of inhabiting *and* rupturing this episteme with our known and un/imaginable lives. (Sharpe 2016: 18)

26. To quote Hartman from the beginning of *Lose Your Mother*:

> If slavery persists as an issue in the political life of black America, it is not because of an antiquarian obsession with bygone days or the burden of a too-long memory, but because black lives are still imperilled and devalued by a racial calculus and a political arithmetic that were entrenched centuries ago. This is the afterlife of slavery—skewed life chances, limited access to health and education, premature death, incarceration, and impoverishment. I, too, am the afterlife of slavery. (Hartman 2021b: 6)

27. Or counter-magical insofar as it is pitched against the realism and reality production of agribusiness writing:

> I have long felt that agribusiness writing is more magical than magic ever could be and that what is required is to counter the purported realism of agribusiness writing with apotropaic writing as countermagic, apotropaic from the ancient Greek meaning the use of magic to protect one from harmful magic. (Taussig 2010: 32–33)

28. See also, for example, Taussig's reflections on his own drawings from his fieldwork notebooks in *I Swear I Saw This* (Taussig 2011).
29. See also my discussion of the map and other details in Russell Hoban's *Riddley Walker* in 'Fictioning a Pilgrimage (Fieldwork on the Fiction of the Self)' (O'Sullivan 2022). Hoban's book also foregrounds the way in which syntax and language can be performative and so are part of this play between reality and fiction.
30. This is similar to how Wark has recently figured autowriting (or what she now also calls 'autotextual writing'): 'The most interesting autotextual writing does one of two things, or even better, both: shows how selves are made, and makes room for a kind of self that otherwise barely gets to exist' (Wark 2023: n. p.).

References

Acker, Kathy and M. Wark (2015), *I'm Very into You: Correspondence 1995-1996*, New York: Semiotext(e).
Atkinson, Terry (2017), *The AGMOAS is now a Corporate Audit*, ed. M. Poole, London: kynastonmcshine.

Barthes, Roland (1975), *S/Z*, trans. R. Miller, London: Jonathan Cape.
——— (1979) *A Lover's Discourse: Fragments*, trans. R. Howard, New York: Farrar, Straus & Giroux.
Barton, Justin (2015), *Hidden Valleys: Haunted by the Future*, Winchester: Zero Books.
Baxter, Katherine and C. Auburn (2023), 'Introduction', special Issue on 'Autotheory in Contemporary Visual Arts Practice', *Arts*, 12.11: 1–8. Available at: https://doi.org/10.3390/arts12010011 (accessed 12 November 2023).
Bellamy, Dodie (2015), 'When the Sick rule the World', *When the Sick Rule the World*, Cambridge, MA: Semiotext(e), pp. 25-36.
Burroughs, William (2008), *The Job: Interviews with William S. Burroughs*, with D. Odier, London: Penguin.
Burrows, David and S. O'Sullivan (2019), *Fictioning: The Myth-Functions of Contemporary Art and Philosophy*, Edinburgh: Edinburgh University Press.
Cixous, Hélène (1981), 'The Laugh of the Medusa', trans. K. Cohen and P. Cohen, *Signs*, 1.4: 875–93 (reprinted in *New French Feminisms: An Anthology*, E. Marks and I. de Courtivron [eds.], Hemel Hempstead: Harvester Wheatsheaf, pp. 245–64).
Colquhoun, Matt (2023), *Narcissus in Bloom: An Alternative History of the Selfie*, London: Repeater.
Deleuze, Gilles (1989), *Cinema 2: The Time-Image*, trans H. Tomlinson and R. Galeta, London: Athlone Press.
Fournier, Lauren (2021), *Autotheory as Feminist Practice in Art, Writing and Criticism*, Massachusetts: MIT Press.
Fournier, Lauren and M. Wark (2020), 'Lauren Fournier and McKenzie Wark on autotheory', MIT Podcast. Available at: https://mitpress.podbean.com/e/full-version-lauren-fournier-and-mckenzie-wark-on-autotheory/ (accessed 30 November 2023).
Gallop, Jane (2002), *Anecdotal Theory*, Durham, US: Duke University Press.
Grant, Catherine and K. R. Love (2019), *Fandom as Methodology: A Sourcebook for Artists and Writers*, London: Goldsmiths Press.
Guattari, Félix (1989), *Schizoanalytic Cartographies*, trans. A. Goffey, London: Bloomsbury.
Gumbs, Alexis Pauline (2020a), *Dub: Finding Ceremony*, Durham: Duke University Press.
——— (2020b), *Undrowned: Black Feminist Lessons from Marine Mammals*, Chico, California: AK Press.

Haraway, Donna (1988), 'Situated Knowledges: The Science Question in Feminism and the Privilege of Partial Perspective', *Feminist Studies*, 14.3: 575–99.

Hartman, Saidiya (2021a), *Wayward Lives, Beautiful Experiments*, London: Serpents Tail.

———— (2021b), *Lose Your Mother: A Journey Along the Atlantic Slave Route*, London: Serpent's Tail.

Hattrick, Alice (2023), *Ill Feelings*, London: Fitzcarraldo.

Heartscape, Porpentine Charity (2016), *Psycho Nymph Exile*, London: Arcadia Missa.

Hedva, Johanna (2015), 'Sick Woman Theory'. Available at: https://johanna-hedva.com/SickWomanTheory_Hedva_2020.pdf (accessed 30 November 2023).

Ireland, Amy (2017) 'The Poememenon: Form as Occult Technology', *Urbanomic Documents*. Available at: https://www.urbanomic.com/document/poememenon/ (accessed 5 September 2021).

Jacques, Juliet (2019), *Trans: A Memoir*, London: Verso.

Kraus, Chris (2006), *I Love Dick*, New York: Semiotext(e).

———— (2017), *After Kathy Acker*, New York: Semiotext(e).

Laing, Olivia (2018), *Crudo*, London: Picador.

Long Chu, Andrea (2019), *Females*, London: Verso.

Lourde, Audre (1982), *Zami: A New Spelling of My Name*, Watertown, MA: Persephone Press.

Negarestani, Reza (2008), *Cyclonopedia: Complicity with Anonymous Materials*, Melbourne: re.press.

Nelson, Maggie (2016), *The Argonauts*, London: Melville House.

O'Sullivan, Simon (2022), 'Fictioning a Pilgrimage (or Fieldwork on the Fiction of the Self)', *Fieldwork for Future Ecologies: Radical Practice for Art and Art-based Research*, eds. B. Crone, S. Nightingale and P. Stanton, Eindhoven: Onomatopee, pp. 397-415.

———— (2024), *From Magic and Myth-Work to Care and Repair*, London: Goldsmiths Press.

Pester, Holly (2015), *Go to Reception and Ask for Sara in Red Felt Tip*, London: Book Works.

———— (2017), 'Archive Fan-Fiction: Experimental Archive Research Methodologies and Feminist Epistemological Tactics', *Feminist Review*, 115.1: 114–29. Available at https://doi.org/10.1057/s41305-017-0042-2 (accessed 27 August 2023).

Preciado, Paul B. (2013), *Testo Junkie: Sex, Drugs, and Biopolitics in the Pharmacopornographic Era*, trans. B. Benderson, New York: The Feminist Press.

——— (2021), *Can the Monster Speak?*, trans. F. Wynne, London: Fitzcarraldo.

Rose, Gillian (1995), *Love's Work*, London: Chatto and Windus.

Sames, Lucy A (2023), *Journal of Writing in Creative Practice*, 16.1 (special issue on 'Ways of Writing in Art and Design II').

Stupart, Linda (2016), *Virus*, London: Arcadia Missa.

Sycamore, Mattilda Bernstein (2020), *The Freezer Door*, New York: Semiotext(e).

Tsing, Anna Lowenhaupt (2015), *The Mushroom at End of the World: On the Possibility of Life in Capitalist Ruins*, Princeton: Princeton University Press.

Sharpe, Christina (2016), *In the Wake: On Blackness and Being*, Durham and London: Duke University Press.

Taussig, Michael (2010), 'The Corn Wolf: Writing Apotropaic Texts', *Critical Inquiry*, 37. 1: 26–33.

——— (2011), *I Swear I Saw This*, Chicago: Chicago University Press.

Wark, McKenzie (2023), 'Critical (Auto) Theory', *e-flux*, 140. Available at: https://www.e-flux.com/journal/140/572300/critical-auto-theory/ (accessed 30 November 2023).

——— (2021), *Philosophy for Spiders: On the Low Theory of Kathy Acker*, Durham, US: Duke University Press.

——— (2020a), 'Girls Like Us', *The White Review*. Available at: https://www.thewhitereview.org/feature/girls-like-us/) (accessed 30 November 2023).

——— (2020b), *Reverse Cowgirl*, New York: Semiotext(e).

4

On Art Writing

Abstract My third essay attempts a tentative definition of—and offers up some propositions for—art writing. It begins by demarcating this genre or field of practice from other forms of writing in and around art—in section (1) Precursors and Fellow Travellers. It then goes on to build its argument through eight further themes or propositions: (2) Pitch, Process and Performance. In which I suggest that art writing tends towards the staged or the self-conscious. (3) Scripts, Spells and Voice. In which art writing is seen to often involve performative modes of expression. (4) Other Registers. Here I look to how art writing can involve other forms of representation besides the written word (for example, drawings or found images). (5) Fictioning and the Foregrounding of Method. In which I suggest that art writing often foregrounds imagery and the imagination, especially in terms of conjuring other space-times. (6) Artists' Books and Novels. In this section, I make the claim that the presentation—in physical form—is important with art writing. (7) Technological Mediations. Here I briefly address art writing in relation to digitalisation and the web. (8) Sites, Scenes and Discursive Communities. In which I address the way in which art writing is often linked to certain sites of publication/distribution and to different scenes. (9) Marked Bodies and a Minor Genre. In this final section, I suggest that art writing can also be a place for marginalised and marked authors and communities (which

© The Author(s), under exclusive license to Springer Nature Switzerland AG 2024
S. O'Sullivan, *On Theory-Fiction and Other Genres*,
https://doi.org/10.1007/978-3-031-65072-7_4

means it resonates with autofiction and autotheory). These themes/propositions are followed by two codas. The first attends to the art collective I am part of as a case study of art writing, specifically in relation to performance; the second and longer one attends to the possibility that art writing (and indeed theory-fiction) might contribute to the project of decolonisation.

Keywords Art Writing • Artist's Book • Performance Fiction • Experimental Writing • Autofiction • Fictioning

Precursors and Fellow Travellers

If there is such thing as art writing, then a first task in defining it would be to demarcate it from other practices of writing in and around art.[1] These latter include art history and theory—perhaps best called writing *on* art—and then also art criticism which, in some of its more experimental forms, can have an affinity with art writing.[2] Key here are artists' own writings, be it as part of their practice or about their practice (or even, perhaps, about other artists' practices). There is a long history of artists' writing in this sense—whether singly or as groups—going back to modernism/the avant-garde, as for example, with various manifestos or, more generally—and beyond modernism—with artists reflecting on their work (or planning future works). As far as writing as part of a practice goes, we can also identify certain precursors to the contemporary scene, perhaps most obviously with conceptual art. In this case, writing is certainly used to communicate ideas, but conceptual art also often foregrounds language as material (as with Lawrence Weiner, for example) or the performative aspect of language (as with Sol LeWitt's instructions or, more obliquely, some of the 'script' texts of the group Art and Language). In relation to this, there is also the artist's book which is a clear pre-cursor of art writing and overlaps with it (indeed, in what follows I am often concerned with art writing specifically as it is presented in books).[3] Reaching further back, this attention to the materiality of language and to performativity is also in play with Dada, where language—used in a certain way (pitched against meaning)—is treated as material, both as phonetic and as asignifying blocks in performances and as found collage material.[4]

Is art writing different to all these cases? On the one hand, it would seem to overlap with many of the fields of writing outlined above and, indeed, partake of many of the same techniques and strategies (certainly there is often an attention to the materiality of language and process, for example). But, on the other, in contemporary examples of art writing, there does seem to be something a little different at stake.

As well as these artistic pre-cursors and fellow travellers, there are also those literary practices that tend towards the experimental and that need to be considered when thinking about art writing and its pre-cursors and parallels.[5] One can look here to texts—and especially fictions—that play with syntax and structure or otherwise foreground their style or involve formal innovation. A key example is William Burroughs and the cut-up method which, like Dada, treats language as material—albeit, with Burroughs, the results are more carefully edited (see as indicative Burroughs's Nova trilogy and especially *Naked Lunch* [1969]). Certainly, Burroughs recognised Tristram Tzara, alongside Brion Gysin, as a key antecedent to the development of his own method.[6] More generally, there are texts that are performative in some manner, either playing with the authorial voice or simply foregrounding their status as texts as, for example, with Kathy Acker's *Blood and Guts in High School* (1984). Then there are also more poetic traditions and practices which experiment with language in a performative manner, as, for example, with concrete poetry. As David Berridge suggests in *Man Arg!*, his own insightful work—and short survey—of art writing (or 'recent convergence of experimental writing and art practice'), other important precursors here are Fluxus and writers like Francis Ponge and Roland Barthes (Berridge 2013: 85).[7] These literary and performative aspects of writing certainly seem to be a key characteristic or resource of some art writing, as we shall see below.

Although less pronounced, there is also genre writing—especially Science Fiction—which is also often a signature of at least some art writing (hence the importance of a writer like Ursula K. Le Guin, who, as we have seen, is also an important precursor to theory-fiction). See, for example, Tai Shani's *Our Fatal Magic* (2019), which looks back to Le Guin and a wider history of feminist Science Fiction. Genre writing can flout some of the rules of narrative—and of characterisation, and so forth—of the typical novel, although it also tends to a certain realism (in terms of 'world-building' and consistency across subjective experiences of those imagined set-ups). Crucially, however, Science Fiction's 'setting' is not the world as it is or, put differently, Science Fiction gestures to an elsewhere. Art writing can make a similar gesture—as if it sometimes operates as a lens on to other worlds. More particularly, art writing, it seems to me, often moves between an avant-garde poetics (or a focus on experimental poetics more generally) and a kind of genre writing. It is often positioned at the edge of different genres in this sense (or, to say the same differently, can flout the rules of a given genre). A book like J. G. Ballard's *The Atrocity Exhibition* (1993 [1970]) seems a key precursor in this respect insofar as it certainly gestures to an elsewhere but is also located at the edge of the Science Fiction genre, especially insofar as it plays with style, structure and presentation.[8] Ballard's novels operate as a lens through which we see a different world or, at least, see our own contemporary world differently (hence the term 'Ballardian'). But a book like *The Atrocity Exhibition* also foregrounds its status *as* a lens or mediating device.[9] It is also worth noting here that Ballard was a key influence on a more direct antecedent to contemporary art writing—one that also involved treating text as material—namely, the writing of Robert Smithson.[10] In fact, the influence was reciprocal. In relation to *Spiral Jetty*, for example, Smithson owned a copy of Ballard's *The Voices of Time* (1960), in which there is the construction of a huge mandala in a salt lake; Ballard then writes a Science Fiction narrative about the *Spiral Jetty*, speculating about what alien cargo might be unloaded there (Ballard 2000). Smithson's writings also turn to Science Fiction more generally, as for example is the case with his comments in 'Entropy and the New Monuments' (1996a) about the way his contemporaries look to Science Fiction films as resource. But Smithson's writings also science *fiction* the work of other artists such as Donald Judd ('The first time I saw Don Judd's "pink plexiglass box", it suggested a giant crystal from another planet' [Smithson 1996b: 7]). In many of these essays, there is also a combination of seriousness/rigour and lightness/humour that gestures forwards towards art writing.

Then there are those other forms of art writing which more readily move away from these 'bachelor stories' as, for example, with art writing that leans towards autofiction/theory or a book like Linda Stupart's *Virus* (2016) that involves a critique of patriarchal and heteronormative values and practices in and of the art world (and academia) as part of its narrative (I will return more than a few times to this text by Stupart). I looked at some of these modes of auto writing in the previous essay, but to repeat a key point in this context, this kind of writing can foreground the narratives of 'marked' subjects (as McKenzie Wark calls them [Wark 2020]). More generally, there is an imbrication here of the personal and the theoretical that we also find in some theory-fiction (once again, the different genres I address in my book are nothing if not blurred; something I will briefly return to in my Conclusion). In terms of our relationship with the non-human (when this includes the non-living), there are also examples of art writing which foreground non-human agents and agencies, such as the two books by the Confraternity of Neoflaggelants (Norman Hogg and Neil Mulholland)—*thN Lng folk 2go: Investigating Future Premoderns* (2013) and *Pan-Pan* (2021)—which also involve a play with style and syntax and, as such, foreground the idea of writing as its own kind of agency. This returns us to some of those texts I looked at in 'On Theory-Fiction'—for example, those by Donna Haraway—that attend specifically to our relation with the non-human. I will look to a couple of further recent case studies of this kind of art writing—examples that also lean towards theory-fiction—in a coda to this essay.

These three aside—(1) Writing by artists (especially as part of their practice); (2) Experimental/genre fiction; and (3) Autotheory and theory-fiction (all of which, when it comes down to it, can be seen within art writing)—are there further characteristics specific to the genre of art writing (if it is one)? What follows are some definitions and propositions—and some examples from the current scene alongside various precursors from the late 1990s onwards. The latter date is a more or less arbitrary starting point but reflects my own awareness and closer involvement with contemporary art discourse from the mid-1990s. My take on art writing draws in texts from this period which might be understood as precursors to art writing, at least as named by Fusco in the early 2000s, alongside more recent examples (post-Fusco as it were).[11] Even more so than the previous essays, what follows is a sampling of an ever-growing and very amorphous field and, with that, a very tentative attempt at working out what art writing is and what it does. And, once again, it is a highly subjective take on this field of writing which arises from the scenes of art writing with which I am most familiar.

Pitch, Process and Performance

Art writing, it seems to me, tends towards the staged or the self-conscious in some manner. There is something here about a text that knows it's a text and plays with this knowledge or self-awareness. Another way of putting this is that art writing is part of an art practice (rather than a literary genre), which means, in David Burrows and Robert Garnett's terms, it is knowingly 'pitched' in a certain manner (see Garnett and Hunt 2008). Or, put differently, and as David Berridge suggests, it has a theatricality to it, both in the sense of individual works utilising dramatic forms—and inviting actual performance—and insofar as art writing is itself a kind of scene of dramatisation (Berridge 2013). An example here—of both this pitch and theatricality—is Joanne Tatham and Tom O'Sullivan's *The Slapstick Mystics with Sticks* (2002), which also had an iteration as a script which was then performed as a play; and their more recent *The Bitter Cup* (2019) that concerns writing and the visual and is, in part, about fictioning a scene of art production. These two books also foreground or frame the genres they are partially within (they play with the novel form) as well as gesturing to an outside of those genres (which is to say they are as involved in thinking through different codes and forms of representation). The pitch and theatricality of art writing can also mean it sometimes takes on a comic tone, as for example, with some of Heather Phillipson's writings that are situated on the border between art and poetry as well as between the body and writing. A good example here is *Not an Essay* (2012), which is a 'Nervous System writing' (to use that phrase from Michael Taussig I turned to in the previous essays) if ever there was one, and which operates as a lens through which we see our own world differently. Another example is Holly Pester's *Go to Reception and ask for Sara in Red Felt Tip* (2015) that is also a kind of fictioned autowriting (or an 'archive fan fiction' as Pester calls it). Both of these examples—the Phillipson and the Pester—also emphasise the importance of presentation and the overall design aspect of art writing, especially in the book form (something I will return to below). Phillipson's writing is also more directly connected to her art practice and, in relation to this essay, to performance.

Another take on this self-aware and comic character—this time from a more counter-cultural perspective (and one which brings the genre of pornography into relation to art writing)—is Stewart Home's *69 Things to do with a Dead Princess* (2002) or the more recent *Blood Rites of the Bourgeoise* (2010). Here the comic is also used to puncture genre (and pretension), for example in art world speak or theory speak. There is also a play in these books with different modes of presentation (for example, the use of the epistolatory form) and with the authorial voice/mode of address. Home's books demonstrate the connections that art writing can have with agitprop scenes and, as such, this kind of art writing also relates to what I briefly suggested in my first essay about the relationship between theory-fiction and, for example, Situationist texts. John Russell's various essays and other writings that move from art writing to theory-fiction (and to art theory more generally) also perform this critique of genre and its associated institutions. They also explore and experiment with the performative aspects of language—see, for example, the different essays collected in *DOGGO* (2017) and his own polemic about art writing (Russell 2012). Russell—like Home—also at times performs his texts. Another example of art writing that is framed or self-conscious—or that plays with (or against) genre—is Katrina Palmer's *The Dark Object* (2010), a fictioned account of an art college experience where real characters interact with fictional ones. Again, this example of art writing also plays with authorial voice and different modes of presentation (forms, memorandums and so forth).

Art writing can also involve a text that plays with the forms and constraints of language more generally or experiments with different modes of presentation (so another nod to avant-garde poetics but, perhaps, less serious or, at any rate, lighter). Berridge's account of works like this—especially those that foreground the process of reading and writing (or give instructions and directions on this)—is especially informative and I encourage any reader interested in this kind of more formally experimental art writing to look out his *Man Arg!* that I mentioned above (a book about art writing that is itself an example of it). Nearly all of my examples so far (and many that follow) are published by Book Works, perhaps the key publisher of art writing in the UK. Indeed, the place of publication and production of art writing is a further crucial aspect to it. I will return to this below.

Scripts, Spells and Voice

Leading on from the above—and from some of the comments I made in my introduction to this essay—art writing is also often more directly performative. It can, for example, involve scripts, as with the Tatham and O'Sullivan book I mentioned above or, as with Maria Fusco's *Master Rock* (2015) present a text (and images) for a performance—in this case at (or inside) Ben Cruachan in Scotland. Another example here is Linda Stupart and Carl Gent's published script for a performance at the ICA in London (as part of an exhibition on the work of Kathy Acker), *All Us Girls Have Been Dead for So Long* (Stupart and Gent 2021). Works of art writing might also contain instructions to the reader, as in Neil Chapman's *Glossolaris* (2010) (published by AND) that proposes a 'diagonal reading' method, resulting in fragments that then produce different scenes and scenarios. As Chapman remarks (in relation to the Science Fiction novel *Solaris* that works as a prompt, of sorts, for his work): 'Like phenomena witnessed on the surface of a remote planet, narratives emerge' (Chapman 2010).[12] It might even involve spells, as in Linda Stupart's *Virus* (2016) (the Stupart and Gent/Stupart books are both published by the gallery-based press Arcadia Missa). In terms of spells (and protocols for rituals more generally) and in relation to an art writing that moves towards poetry—or a poetry that moves towards art writing—see also the work of trans poet CAConrad (for example, *Ecodeviance* [2014]). Indeed, it can often be the case that art writing announces both a theatrical and magical operation of writing in this sense. There is a connection here with a kind of strategy of acting/performing and writing 'as if' something is already the case. Or, put differently, there is the use of a fictional mode of address so as to call forth something else. An interesting case study here—of writing having this magical effect—is sigil magick (see the discussion [in relation to Austin Osman Spare] in Burrows and O'Sullivan 2019: 70-71).

More broadly, art writing (like theory-fiction) seems to involve texts that perform their content in some manner or where the performative character of a text is foregrounded. An example of this is the *Dialecty* publishing project initiated by Maria Fusco (once again with the UK Artists' books publisher Book Works). Fusco's editorial project, consisting of a number of short pamphlet/books by different writers, 'considers the uses of vernacular forms to explore how dialect words, grammar and syntax challenge and improve traditional orthodoxies of critical writing' (Fusco 2018). This also relates to my comments above regarding how art writing will often deploy a number of different forms and styles or bring two or more genres into conjunction. As far as the latter goes—bringing different genres into encounter—see also Francesco Pedraglio's art writing, for example, *Battles, Vol. 1* (2021), which presents a series of scenarios of different kinds as well as, once again, scripts for different kinds of performance. In terms of the former—the mobilising of different forms and styles of writing (and a play with syntax and presentation more generally)—see, for example, Kit Poulson's *The Ice Cream Empire* (2012) and the later *Mutter* (the result of a residency at a library and the presentation of 'a book like a synthesizer' [Poulson 2018, ix]).

Related to this performative aspect—and linking art writing to autofiction/theory—there is also often the use of the first-person pronoun or a thematising of the author within the text, as in Hannah Black's collection of fiction/non-fiction writings *Dark Pool Party* (Black 2017) or Sophia Al-Maria's *Sad Sack* (Al-Maria 2019). As with some autowriting more generally, here the use of a certain style and first-person narrative foregrounds the importance of individual experience and of a subjective/situated perspective. In these kinds of text, however, the foregrounding of the I is more staged, or more theatrical, than in some of the examples I looked at in the previous chapter. In relation to one of the key themes of my own book we might say that there is a kind of framing of the fiction of the self with this art writing, as well as the presentation of other fictions of other selves. This kind of play with authorship and fiction can be found in some of John Russell's art writing, such as *Head*, another Book

Works title, which Russell wrote under the pseudonym Mo-Leeza Roberts and in which he engages with the art world through the device of the quasi-fictional Head Gallery (Roberts 2015). Experimenting with ideas of authorship and with what might be called authorial 'voice'—especially in a performative manner—seems to be a key gesture of art writing.

Other Registers

Art writing also often involves other registers and forms of representation besides the written word, including drawings or found images (or even, in some cases, maps or diagrams). Hence the importance of a writer like Kathy Acker, and especially the novel I mentioned above, *Blood and Guts in High School* (1984), that contains her dream maps and other drawings.[13] Another example, here, would be Stupart's book *Virus*, which I have also mentioned above (Stupart 2016) and which implicitly looks back to Kathy Acker (not least in its use of different typefaces alongside the inclusion of drawings) and also Gent and Stupart's book, which also includes images—photos of the performance and reproduced drawings—alongside the script (Stupart and Gent 2021). A further example is Sophia Al-Maria's book—also mentioned above—which includes photographs, found images and screenshots interspersed amongst the texts, some of which are themselves more performative in character (Al-Maria 2019). There is also the drawings in Francisco Pedraglio's *Battles, vol. 1* (2021) that I mentioned above or the photos (and other forms of presentation) in Ole Hagen's *Nowhere Less Now* (Hagen 2012), a fiction written for Lindsey Seers' Artangel project *The Tin Tabernacle*, but which, in part, looks back to a writer like W. G. Sebald in its use of images and text.[14] In both these latter cases—Pedraglio and Hagen—the books gesture to other works and/or performances outside of themselves (so to a register 'beyond' the text and, to a certain extent, beyond representation too).

An example of an artist who uses diagrams in and as part of their art writing (and wider) practice is David Osbaldeston. See, for example,

Inflection Sandwich (2015), which presents diagrams as a mode of artistic thinking and as metaphysical fictioning device. Osbaldeston's practice involves tracking across different registers of representation, as well as using text (and theory) in and as a performative mode.

More generally, there is an emphasis in art writing on non-standard formats and layouts as well as different fonts and text sizes (so the general 'look' of a given text). This is in play with many of the examples above and relates also to a whole history of experimentation with text and typefaces as well as of text and image and how they have been brought together—to work with or against each other—in different manuscripts and publications. All of this connects with what I have briefly said above in relation to precursors to art writing (especially within avant-garde poetics), but it also links art writing to other experiments across the written and visual. There is a separate and more literary history to be written here, one that especially turns to the British Poetry Revival, for example, but also goes way back to before these modern and contemporary precursors, for example to attend to the way text and image are used within medieval manuscripts.[15] In fact, there seems to be a link here between contemporary art writing and these pre-modern writing/image practices as also evidenced in the books by the Confraternity of Neoflagellants that I mentioned above and, indeed, in David Berridge's continuing fictioned enquiry into experimental art writing practices that involve the invented persona of a medieval illuminator (Hugo Pictor).

There are many different artists and other scenes (and accounts of both) where experimentation with writing and image takes place. To point to just one more—in relation to what I say about the genre of Science Fiction in my introduction to this essay—there were the artists and writers involved in *Ambit* journal, including J. G. Ballard and Eduardo Paolozzi. Here text and image combination and the look of the magazine were as important as the genre-pushing fiction. To return to art witing per se, what can be said, more generally, and in relation to this section on 'Other Registers' is that the visual (in whatever form) is very often important to art writing.

Fictioning and the Foregrounding of Method

In so far as it is part of an art practice, art writing often foregrounds imagery and the imagination over concepts and theory (and so is more akin to straightforward fiction than, for example, theory-fiction). This is not always the case. Indeed, in some examples of art writing (or the experimental bringing together of art and writing), it is the conceptual that is foregrounded (as in conceptual art itself). But it does seem to be the case that with many examples of contemporary art writing images are conjured through description or, more generally, the imagination as faculty is engaged. A key precursor here is Clarice Lispector's writing (see, for example, *Água Viva* [2014 (1973)])—also a key precursor to autofiction—or, more obliquely, books by Anna Kavan (and especially the novel *Ice* [2017 (1967)] that the novelist Christopher Priest describes as producing 'a sense of "otherness" in the audience, like a glimpse into a distorting mirror' [Priest 2021: n. p.]).[16] A more contemporary example is the fantastical images and scenarios in Tai Shani's *Our Fatal Magic* (published by Strange Attractor), which also, crucially, derives from a performance. This foregrounding of imagination—the distorting mirror—also relates to the way art writing can have a closer affinity to genre writing such as Science Fiction—again, as I mentioned in my Introduction—and especially with the more experimental works from within (or at the edge) of that genre.

Moving in the other direction, and to return to a point I made in the previous section, there is also that art writing that looks to the past, as for example with Huw Lemmy's *Unknown Language* (Bingen and Lemmy 2020) that actually involves the traversing across multiple times in its tale of the female mystic Hildegard of Bingen (and also involves a collaboration with Bhanu Kapil and Alice Spawls). There is also that writing that has become known as 'Neomedievalism' as, for example, once again, with the two books by the Confraternity of Neoflaggelants I have mentioned a couple of times and which also demonstrate once again the importance of a performative style of art writing (and, in this case, a kind of mixed up future-past syntax and grammar). Might we say in this respect that art writing finds its resources and perspectives in different places but also in different times? More generally, and to bring in an idea David Burrows and I discuss elsewhere (Burrows and O'Sullivan 2019)—and which I have already turned to in previous essays here—there is a *fictioning* of materials with art writing, which here denotes a certain treatment of text so it has a staged feel to it (in relation to the above, we might say there is a fictioning of the future or the past). A further example here would be the *Communiquè 4* booklet by Alun Rowlands that is about—or fictions—a certain scene around the Angry Brigade (Rowlands 2008). This also relates to that art writing that writes on another writer or uses the latter as prompt, for example Sam Keogh's *Impossible Knotworm* (2020) that looks to Doris Lessing's *The Good Terrorist* (Keogh's volume being part of a series of books/pamphlets published by MA Bibliothèque with the title 'The Good Reader').

In fact, leading on from this and what I say about performativity above, it might be that the term 'performance fiction' is suitable for art writing. In our co-written book *Fictioning*, Burrows and I used the term 'performance fiction' to describe the embodiment or materialisation of fiction within reality, but I think it might also be used to refer to this self-conscious deployment of fiction as a kind of method within art writing.[17] What does this method achieve? As well as opening a window onto another world or offering up a different perspective—which in itself can have a political importance in terms of presenting other imaginaries—there is also a sense in which the method itself (the frame as it were) is foregrounded.[18] Could this be a further proposition for and about art writing? That it does what it does but somehow, either explicitly or implicitly, foregrounds its methods?

Artists' Books and Novels

Leading on from this foregrounding of method, the presentation—in physical form—seems especially important with art writing. For example, it is often presented as an artist's book or other kind of artist's publication (pamphlet, zine and so forth). This also relates to the importance of certain presses and places of publication. A good example of this is John Russell's multi-volume *Frozen Tears* anthologies (Russell 2003–2007), published by the Birmingham-based Article Press, which present the book as object—with the size and weight of an airport novel—and which itself gathers together examples of art writing, broadly understood (or even produces a certain scene of art writing). Russell's books self-consciously present art writing in a trashy and 'cheap' format (volumes of *Frozen Tears* are more or less impossible to read without cracking the spine). Again, there is something important in play here about the clashing of different genres. Art writing, as well as having a certain style and being a genre (at least of sorts), has a 'made' character in this sense, in that it foregrounds its existence as object—or even as a kind of 'social object'—as well as text.[19] Hence, once again, the importance—in the UK—of the publisher Book Works and their roster of freelance book designers.[20] Indeed, in many cases, the artists' books produced by Book Works are the result of a three-way collaboration between Book Works, the artists concerned and independent designers (to take three indicative examples of designers from volumes already mentioned: Matt Appleton/Modern Activity and *The Bitter Cup*; James Langdon and *Go to Reception and Ask for Sara in Red Felt Tip*; and Frazer Muggeridge Studio and *Mo-Leeza Roberts: Head*).[21]

In relation to the presentation of art writing within the book form, there is also the 'Artist's novel' as David Maroto calls it. Examples here include *Headless* by K. D. (published by Sternberg), a kind of detective genre novel in which the artists Goldin+Senneby are characters (so a kind of ghost-written autofiction) and which involves the investigation into an offshore financial company named Headless and the connection of that to Bataille's *Acéphale* group (K. D. [Goldin+Senneby] 2014). Acèphale; or Mai Thu Perret's 'The Crystal Land' (published in *Land of Crystal* [Perret 2008]), which is also actualised in different objects and installations by the artist (so here the novel is used by the artist as a prompt for other material instantiations and enactments). Maroto addresses the above two works and other examples of what he sees as a distinct genre in his book on *The Artist's Novel* (Maroto 2019). Crucially, the artist's novel, for Maroto, is not simply a novel written by an artist, but one that is written as part of an artist's practice (so, just as an artist might employ performance or installation or any other 'medium' as part of their practice, so they might also employ the novel form) (see Maroto

2019). Maroto's own artist's novel—that narrates the writing of an artist's novel—is especially interesting here insofar as it foregrounds the metafictional aspect of the artist's novel (see Maroto 2020).

As well as the novel form, art writing might also take on the form of an anthology of writing. A recent example is the publisher Prototype's *Intertitles* (Chandler et al. 2021), produced in collaboration with curators Hana Noorali and Lynton Talbot, in which, again, attention to design and production is of great importance. Indeed, anthologies—alongside journals and magazines—seem a key mode of distribution and dissemination of art writing. As well as this turn to recognisable genres, such as the novel, there is also, once again, that art writing that is more poetic in character or experimental in form and presentation. In fact, this is often the case with many artist's books that attend as much to their form and look as to the content (and also often to the binding, the paper used, process of manufacture and so forth). Once again, Berridge's book on art writing is especially good on this aspect, presenting and describing a variety of examples that foreground their status as made things. In general, then, the presentation and whole look/feel of art writing seems to be important—and, with that, especially the book form. Might we even say that the form and presentation of art writing tend to be part of the content, as it were?

Technological Mediations

The contemporary importance of the artist's book and the book form (and, more generally, of what might be called the physicality of writing) is especially interesting inasmuch as this turn to material production is occurring at the same time as the increasing ubiquity of the digital and of text on the web. Art writing can also involve a response to this, either in the utilisation of these technologies—where it dovetails with what Kenneth Goldsmith calls 'uncreative' or conceptual writing (Goldsmith 2011) and Nathan Allen Jones calls 'glitch poetics' (Jones 2022)—or through a renewed emphasis on the craft and manufacture of the book (for example, with the books produced by Book Works). Goldsmith's book gives a number of examples of writing practices that utilise technological mediations or machine techniques and methods, whilst at the same time pointing to various avant-garde precursors. Although not specific to art writing, Goldsmith is certainly interested in the intersections between art and writing and, more specifically, puts forward the argument that creative writing practices have much to learn from art practice (especially post-Duchamp and Warhol). Jones's book discusses a number of case studies that are closer to the kinds of art writing I have been concerned with, for example, Linda Stupart's *Virus* that I discussed earlier or the writing and performances of Erica Scourti. Indeed, Scourti's book *The Outage* (2014) is an especially interesting example of an art writing that is technologically mediated—and one that gestures back to autowriting (as well as the artist's novel)—insofar as it is a ghost-written memoir (and also a kind of Science Fiction) written or assembled from Scourti's digital footprint (it also contains various images of screen shots to accompany the narrative). For Jones, it is especially practices that mobilise the glitch that are important as this in itself points towards the possibility of new genres of art and writing. An interesting example of the former—of technologically mediated art writing—and one that Jones also discusses is Ryan Trecartin's experimental scriptwriting (see the interview with Trecartin 2011). I will return to this in my coda to this book on 'Machine Writing', but suffice to say here that Trecartin's writing is prompted by new technology, and especially coding and social media. In relation to 'new' technology and the impact on styles of writing see also the interesting experimental collaborations with AI/algorithms, for example Alice Bucknall's 'New Mystics' project, which concerns the collaboration between artists and new AI language systems (or 'Large Language Models'), and which also brings magical notions into relation with technology.[22] This returns us to what I mentioned above about different times being a resource for art writing, but also connects with some of the comments in my essay on theory-fiction about writing and time loops. The 'New Mystics' project also shows how important websites are in the presentation and dissemination of art writing (and also the importance of various blog communities more generally, as I mentioned in my essay on theory-fiction). I look at some more general implications of technology (and especially recent AI systems) for writing—and at what might be called machine writing—in a postscript to my book.

Finally in this section on technological mediations, it is worth mentioning the new print-on-demand technologies which mean cheaper publishing can happen away from the usual big publishers and gatekeepers. This has an impact, at least to some extent, on the range of writing out there. There is also the way in which what is called 'The Long Tail' of the internet brings a readership/market to more niche publications (certainly new communities of readers are called forth by this technologically enabled scene of publication). In general then, different scenes of art writing respond creatively to technological mediation in different ways as well as sometimes themselves being called forth by new technologies.

Sites, Scenes and Discursive Communities

To be more explicit about something already mentioned above, art writing—like theory-fiction—is often characterised by its links to certain sites of publication. Five key examples in the UK are Book Works (which, as I have already mentioned, publishes artist's books); Sharon Kivland's MA Bibliothèque (which publishes essays and fictions by artists and others); Strange Attractor (which publishes at the intersection of 'unpopular culture' and magic); Prototype (which publishes fiction and more interdisciplinary and performative texts and, develops out of Jess Chandler's previous project, Test Centre, that also looks back to the scene around the British Poetry Revival mentioned briefly above); and Ignota books (which publishes fiction and non-fiction at the intersection of magic, technology and ecology).[23] I mention these five as they are the ones I am most familiar with or which have the most prominence in the scenes I am most familiar with. There are many other independent presses in the UK that also publish what might be called art writing, for example, Penned in the Margins that published Heather Phillipson's *This Is Not an Essay* (2012) which I have already mentioned above; or, the more mainstream and prolific, Fitzcarraldo Editions that, for example, publishes some of Ed Atkins's writings such as *A Primer for Cadavers* (2016), a volume that includes his drawings—and other plays with form and presentation— alongside the poetic (or non-poetic) writing.[24]

Art writing can also be linked to certain sites and circuits of distribution or dissemination (besides online or direct from the publishers). In

London, for example, there was X Marks the Bökship (once again, see Berridge's book that is an account of a reading residency there) and still is Tender Books and Banner Repeater (the latter containing perhaps the key archive of art writing, certainly in the UK). The latter are also important sites for the publication/production of texts and for the performance (and discussion) of art writing (for example, the bookshop Berridge had a residency at had a Riso printer and was a performance space as well as a bookshop).[25] In Glasgow, there is The Good Press that also prints books. Other examples are After 8 Books in Paris and Motto in Berlin. Indeed, it is mainly within independent bookshops that we find art writing that is itself produced by independent presses (and galleries).[26] To repeat the crucial point made above, this means art writing is partly determined by its location on the fringes and margins of more typical—and dominant— literary cultures (and their associated bookshops). It also means that art writing has a relationship with other hybrid forms of writing and/or writing by other non-white, queer—or indeed working class—writers. I will return to this crucial aspect below. I will also briefly look at three further non-UK publishers in my coda to this essay.

As well as the above sites of publication, art writing more generally involves different scenes or other discursive communities. It is writing that is both *from* and *for* this community of interest (as well as helping to form these scenes). This also means that artists themselves often take control of the mode of production (and distribution) of their books and other publications.[27] See, for example, artist-led writing projects such as the *Art-Writing-Research* book series initiated by David Burrows (himself a prolific art writer) and published by Article Press in Birmingham (Burrows et al. 2011)—and the launch of the five books at an important event at X Marks the Bökship in 2011. Article Press are a key precursor to the present scene of art writing and also demonstrate that what might be called art writing was happening well before this term was coined. There are also different journals and magazines that are produced by artists and collectives, such as the *Inventory* journals (1995–2005) (also the name of the art collective that produced the publications) and (more recently) *Rattle* (where early iterations of Holly Pester's archive-fiction was published) (2010–15) in London, or *British Mythic* (1998–2001), *STOPSTOP* (1997/1999) and (more recently) *Uncle Chop Chop* (2002–2016) in

Glasgow. Not all of these examples would describe themselves as art writing, but, certainly, they exhibit many of the characteristics I have laid out in my above propositions. Art writing might be seen as an ongoing conversation in this sense or as a 'sociable writing' to use David Berridge's term (Berridge 2013: 8).[28] This also relates to the comments I made towards the beginning of this essay insofar as it means this writing has a pitch or positionality to it. Indeed, it is in this sense, to repeat a point I made earlier, that art writing is part of contemporary art practice rather than literature per se (although that is not to deny the various traverses and blurrings of that border, too). Within art writing there are invariably further scenes that I have not touched upon here (and scenes within scenes). There is also a further sense—again identified by Berridge—in which an idea of scenes (and scripts) is important in terms of describing art writing more generally, with its different 'locations, actions, and characters' (Berridge 2013: 12). There is, as it were, a general scene of art writing. Once again, we return to a key theme of my own book: the performance of fictions and other texts (including, here, the fictioning of a scene or different scenes).

Marked Bodies and Minor Genre

Finally, and leading on from what I say above about discursive communities—and scenes within scenes—art writing, perhaps most crucially, can also be from and for communities that are more marginalised or marked, or that are positioned away from mainstream literary and/or academic communities. This has been implicit in some of what I have already laid out in this essay—for example, in the turn to feminist writings and perspectives and/or auto styles—but it also relates directly to queer and trans writing (which, once again, is why there are the close affinities between art writing and autowriting) or indeed 'crip' writing and theory (see, for example, my brief comments on 'Sick Woman Theory' in my previous essay, 'On Autofiction and Autotheory'). Here the performative and experimental nature of art writing is part of any project/claim insofar as it calls a community—or scene—forth at the same time as it is set against patriarchal and or heteronormative genres and styles (of literary expression and writing more generally). Art writing can be a place for this kind of writing that is positioned away from the literary establishment. In this sense, it can also be a home to working-class writers, as Isabel Waidner suggests in their own survey of art writing and account of why she found it more of a welcoming home than other more literary worlds for her experimental fiction (Waidner 2021a). See also Waidner's *Liberating the Canon*, a gathering together of experimental working-class writers (2018), and the recent book by Maria Fusco *Who Does Not Envy Us Is Against Us* (2023) that is, in part, about the challenges of being a working-class writer as well as a working out of what 'working class as method' might mean. I will need to leave it to others to work through in more detail the relationship of class to these new forms and genres of writing (not only the authors, but the readers and also the bookshops and so forth), but what can be said is that mainstream literary culture tends to be the preserve of the middle class and thus working-class writing needs must explore and invent other forms and modes of writing its experiences (and other sites of production and dissemination).

There is also a limit here insofar as art writing is or can be part of the art world with all the issues of entrance and exclusion this involves. But it can also work against these logics to some extent insofar as it is a more distributed mode of cultural production, constituted as it is around 'social objects' as well as different scenes that are positioned away from any over-dominant centres. Once again, then, it is the way in which this genre is in the margins or is a 'minor' genre (to use again that term from Deleuze and Guattari that I discussed in my 'Introduction' to this book) that allows it to speak of other experiences and identities. At the same time, its different styles and modes of presentation allow for a critique of more majoritarian forms of writing (for example, that associated with the 'universal' middle-class, cis-hetero, white, male, able-bodied subject [if not the fiction of the self more generally]). Hannah Black's *Dark Pool Party* is a kind of minor writing in this sense and one that—in its style—blurs the distinction between fiction and non-fiction, as well as that between autowriting and critique. Two other recent examples of what this kind of writing can be—ones that position themselves within, or at the edge of, the genre of Science Fiction—are Orion J. Facey's *Virosexuals* (2021), itself structured around acts and scenes, with the use of different fonts and with a cover by the artist Danielle Braithwaite-Shirley, and Porpentine

Heartscape's *Psycho Nymph Exile Art* that also plays with form and presentation and has a cross-platform transmedial aspect. Both these books involve narratives about a non-heteronormative and trans future community that also works to call the latter forth.[29] As I mentioned in my essay on autowriting, Heartscape's book could also be thought of as a kind of genre-bending autofiction. Art writing dovetails with other genres and, indeed, other scenes of writing and literary experimentation here. A good example of the latter is Isabelle Waidner's work *Gaudy Bauble* (2017) that is innovative in its non-linear narrative, content and style. In relation to some of my comments above, this text also mobilises all kinds of different registers (alongside its formal devices) and includes diagrams, logos and images. It is also here that we need to gesture beyond the writing of books to those other forms of writing—fanzines, samizdat and such like—that are located away even from this genre and which are from and for scenes and communities that would not consider themselves part of any art or literary world. I am thinking here, again, of more countercultural and underground scenes and the writing practices associated with them. In relation to radical politics and music, for example, see the fanzines *Break/flow* and *Datacide*. More generally, the writings of Howard Slater are a good example of this radical—and working class—writing that is both about and performs its thesis of the affective classes (see Slater 2012).[30] In my second coda below, I also extend this final category of 'Marked Bodies and Minor Genre' to look at how art writing (and indeed, theory-fiction) might be more explicitly part of a project of decolonisation (when this also includes addressing the issues of our climate crisis). Before that, however, I want to offer up a first coda that once again foregrounds more of my own situated perspective and personal investment—in this case, on and with art writing.

Coda 1: Plastique Fantastique as Case Study

I am part of an art collective which has, as part of its practice, produced texts that might be described as art writing.[31] In our case, these texts have generally been scripts—or contained protocols—for performances.[32] They have often operated as a kind of platform or scaffolding to allow

other things to occur. Here, the writing has a definite performative character insofar as it contains directions and actions and then, crucially,
speeches. Early Plastique Fantastique scripts were more akin to traditional
mumming plays, albeit with a different and more future-orientated
inflection (in fact, they often involved a kind of made-up future-past
syntax [something, as I remarked above, that is characteristic of
Neomedievalism]). Later scripts have been more involved in a storytelling function (at times connected to ecological themes). In each case,
different characters or avatars had different parts to play (or to channel).
In the performances themselves, various masks and props were used to
further actualise or conjure a given scene and summon further avatars.
Indeed, this was how we understood Plastique Fantastique at that time,
as a kind of 'performance fiction'.

Plastique Fantastique performances tended to use a variety of components and operate on a variety of registers.[33] There would be sonic elements, with different instruments and electronic devices (especially
microphones), as well as audio-visual elements, with the projection of
films and video (often as a kind of backdrop to any performance). And
then there would be the performers themselves who would be speaking
various parts, carrying out the protocols and so forth. The intention was
often to call something else forth, a different entity or egregore perhaps?
Something that was intended but unintended too. There was a sense that
the scripts were partly about this magical function: if not spells exactly,
they were certainly instructions for this summoning.

To focus further on the writing, early texts involved a turn to a pre-
modern vernacular or a bringing of that into encounter with present
modes of popular expression and even future ones (so, once again, a kind
of made-up future-past syntax). Before this we also produced manifestos
for the practice. These were not comic exactly—and they were certainly
involved in the serious work of mapping out a future trajectory—but they
were self-conscious or played with the manifesto form and its various
tropes. It was the first manifesto (written to accompany a solo show by
David Burrows) which, in fact, called Plastique Fantastique into existence
(or actualised the fiction). The text came first and called that which it
named forth (which has also been the case in different performances where
a word or a name operates as the summoning technology). Other

performances were involved in a kind of a mimicking of machinic processes (and a becoming-object more generally). I'll return to this area in my postscript to this book 'On Machine Writing'. More recently, Plastique Fantastique has produced songs and tracks as well as what might be called sonic fictions. I have been less involved in this more recent work, but it seems to me that the different lyrics—so, again, a form of writing—relate to the themes of the performances but also look back, for example to folk traditions, as well as gesturing towards technologically mediated futures (so a turn to other times away from the present).

Crucial is also that these writings were often collaboratively produced (they were from and for a collective, even a scene of sorts). In fact, Plastique Fantastique also produced collaborative fictions that were less tied to performances (although they would mobilise the same set of characters and avatars). Here the texts were not exactly stories—or, if they were, they were ones that involved the avatars of Plastique Fantastique traversing into the fiction as well as a use of images and drawings alongside text. Crucially, these stories were also about 'real-world' events—not least during the pandemic, which also enforced a change in direction for Plastique Fantastique with the shift to performances online.[34] This traversing across scenes and between ontological levels—or between fiction and reality—seems important in terms of the idea of art writing constituting a general scenography (and relates back to some of my comments in the essay on theory-fiction about the nesting of fictions).[35]

Plastique Fantastique has also experimented with other practices that are forms of writing, such as sigils (writing these but also performing them).[36] More recent performances have involved tarot cards.[37] Here the writing, images and general production of the tarot pack is part of the practice (a magician must always make their own tools as the saying goes). Tarot is not art writing, but there is something about the performative nature of the tarot—and the instructions (for example, about the lay) and sets of interpretations, which resonates, again, with some of what I say above in relation to art writing as a performative mode or as involving sets of instructions. And, of course, the tarot is a divinatory technique, which means, once again, that it relates to some of what I have said in my theory-fiction chapter about different methods and devices of writing as a kind of time travel or as the looping of time.

Coda 2: Art Writing as Decolonial Practice

Although I addressed the idea briefly in 'On Theory-Fiction' I want now to turn to those forms of experimental writing—or, at least, writing that plays with form—that might be understood as contributing to the project of decolonisation in some sense. This might be down to the content of such writing, but crucially it is also the style in which it is written and indeed the way this content is presented. Put differently—and to a return to a key theme of these essays—it is how some of this writing performs its content in some manner that seems important (a couple of key examples that I mentioned in my first essay are Stefan Harney and Fred Moten's *The Undercommons* [2013] and Donna Haraway's 'The Camille Stories' in her *Staying with the Trouble* [2016: 134–168]). This longer second coda also gives me the opportunity to review some further and more recent examples of art writing and especially that art writing which blurs with theory-fiction.

In general, then, the writing I have in mind turns away from a more typical academic or scholarly register that often pretends a distanced or objective perspective or assumes a 'universal' view (which, nevertheless, is a white, male, able-bodied, cis-hetero and privileged one). In terms of presentation this is also to sometimes turn away from the standard essay—or monograph form—which, in this context, might be understood as a key aspect of the knowledge economy of institutions such as the university. This might also be understood as a form that itself reflects certain hierarchies and exclusions (and, as part of that, also a Eurocentric attitude to knowledge production). A decolonising practice needs to address the deeper assumptions and structures of these institutions—which also means, in relation to writing, it needs to go beyond any manifest content. Once again, it needs to operate at the level of form; or perform its content in some way.[38]

In my first essay in this book, 'On Theory-Fiction', I wrote about the way that new and hybrid forms of writing can involve a para-academic attitude and 'posture' if not also—following François Laruelle—a radically democratic one. But here I want to suggest that some of the more experimental forms of art writing—especially when more theoretically orientated—can take this further or enact more radical ways of imaging/ presenting difference. Crucial, it seems to me, is that this writing does not simply perform a critique of the business-as-usual of the Academy— so it is not just a turn away (vital though this is)—but presents, performs and produces alternatives (so operates on a more affirmative register). In fact, it is this offering up of alternatives that performs the critique, as it means this writing can foreground other voices and subject positions often left out of the Academy; it thus shows us the boundaries and limits of these more typical forms of knowledge production. Often this kind of writing also situates its author within the text as a specifically political/ ethical gesture (as is also the case with autofiction and autotheory). To put all this slightly differently, these kinds of examples present a scene of difference within other more dominant scenes (and in this sense of opening up or mapping out a scene, these writings and books might also be broadly understood not only as curatorial projects but also as different kinds of perspectival device).[39]

Rather than attempting to demarcate any further principles or formal qualities of this writing as I have done in the above essay (and which, in the context of this coda, might be seen as a gesture of capturing and containing), in what follows I want to briefly look at three case studies of what might be called art writing—but might equally fit the rubric of theory-fiction—as decolonial practice. My three case studies are also linked to three publishers which it seems to me are at the forefront of this sub-genre, if it can be called that (I mention further examples of their books in the accompanying footnotes to this part of my essay). It is also an opportunity to turn away from the predominantly UK context of my art writing examples so far.[40]

An Ongoing-Offcoming Tale (Archive Books). As well as its content— this is a book broadly about contemporary art and decolonisation—the presentation of the writing in *An Ongoing-Offcoming Tale* (Bejeng Ndikung 2022) is different to other books in this field, at least to some extent.[41] The book is structured around five 'Tales' each of which has a title and an associated diagram or pictogram that appears in the contents and then again at the beginning—in a larger size—of each section (Aziza Ahmad is the named designer). Essays—generally written on commission and to accompany exhibitions—are interspersed with conversations.

These conversations are also marked in the contents with a diagram or drawing. Each text also begins with an explanation of when and where it arose and, crucially, who contributed towards the writing of it. The sense is very much that the book is a gathering and, although it is signed only by Bonaventura Soh Bejeng Ndikung, is nonetheless the production of a community (as, indeed, the author also makes clear in the acknowledgements at the end of the volume).[42] This seems crucial in terms of the decentring of knowledge production I mentioned above (the 'sole author' being another one of those key components of typical knowledge production). The essays themselves also experiment more directly with style and presentation, with some of them, for example, sub-divided into 'Acts' or 'Stanzas', which in themselves suggest a more performative and poetic mode (and resonate with some of the art writing I have already mentioned above). Some of the pages also contain QR codes—thus calling for another technical device in order to be activated—taking the reader to various images and other audio-visual material (so the book, literally, gestures to an archive beyond itself).

The book positions itself as an intervention into dominant epistemologies, one that proceeds through 'an approach rooted in an inherent decentring of the ways in which knowledge is understood to be produced' (this is from the back of the book). The book also foregrounds those artistic methods and methodology which are at odds with the more usual objective (and scientific) methods of knowledge production. Indeed, as I suggested above, art writing is defined, at least in one sense, as a form of writing mobilised by artists in a way that is appropriate to their practice. Here it is also a curatorial strategy or, at least, written and edited by a curator whose intention is to follow the method—and modes of knowledge production—of the artistic practices themselves (rather than writing 'on' them as it were).[43]

This book is then an exploration of different artistic (and curatorial) methods and epistemologies.[44] And the style (for example, the play with format or foregrounding of collaboration) and presentation (for example, the use of images and structuring of the book as a journey) is part of this experimental project. Indeed, the book is not only *about* these different practices but is also an expanded account of a particular practice. As I have suggested in my two previous essays, there is something compelling about a book that performs its content or, in this context, a book that is both about art practice and in itself an example of an art practice. Or, to put it in terms of this coda, a book about decolonisation within the expanded field of contemporary art that also—again, at least to some extent—decolonises the modes of production of knowledge (so, once again, it performs its content).

Enfleshed: Ecologies of Entities and Beings (Onamatopee books). This volume also concerns a different form of knowledge production—specifically trans-disciplinary and arising from multi-species ecologies—and, as such, pitches itself against what it calls 'dominant Western perspectives' (Koskentola and Van der Loo 2023: 7). In the words of its editors, 'the volume reflects on interconnectedness and co-creation processes of complex, more-than-human ecologies to address our current socio-political and ecological crisis' (Koskentola and Van der Loo 2023: 7). The book itself consists of different essays, fictions and other forms of writing, as well as photographs, film stills and other images. Attention has been given especially to the overall design, including typefaces and fonts (so the whole 'look' of the book; the graphic designer is Yannick Nuss). As with the previous volume, it uses images—in this case, diagrammatic symbols—to identify each author with a particular landscape or biome. This volume is an example of a kind of art writing that leans towards the theoretical, but it is also, like the previous volume, a record of an ongoing curatorial project.[45]

The inclusion of texts that are more poetic or are fieldwork notes or that attend to shamanic and other ritual practices—presenting them rather than 'interpreting' them—means that it does not reproduce more typical academic knowledge or have the character of more standard academic anthologies.[46] To a certain extent, this book presents the different kinds of non-Western perspectives and knowledge systems which many of the essays are concerned with. As an anthology, it specifically foregrounds the idea of a gathering that was also in play in my previous example. Crucially, however, this volume is not a turn away from modernity but an active engagement with certain aspects of it, bringing our different presents and possible futures into conjunction with different pasts (so there is a connection here with some of what I say above about different futures and pasts being a kind of resource for thinking differently). The thematic list of subjects on the front cover foregrounds the hybrid and syncretic character of its contents, which, once again, is reflected in the different registers and formats used in the volume. It's worth quoting in full: *'Internal alchemy; Siberian perspectivism; Shamanisms; Anti-Cartesianism; Ecofeminism; Quantum Theory; Electromagnetism; Environmentalism; Feminist Sci-Fi; Cosmologies; Mumming; Decoloniality; Poetry-as-Theory; Mythologies; and more'*. It is especially the inclusion of Poetry-as-Theory and subjects such as Mumming—a traditional and performative mode of story-telling—that means this volume leans into art writing.

More generally, the project of decolonisation here is linked to the question of non-human agencies and intelligences and, more broadly, to ecological perspectives and the addressing of ecological issues such as the rampant extractivism in Eurasia.[47] As I mentioned in both my previous essays, addressing these issues of our Anthropocene necessarily means turning to other modes of representation and writing (away from those forms and modes that can be an expression—or weak mode—of more typical knowledge production). Can a book adequately make this turn? It seems to me that *Enfleshed* is as good as any other attempt to use the book form to explore how a scene of difference can be presented between its covers. Some of its texts also lean towards the performative (for example, with the inclusion of transcriptions of indigenous spoken word stories or the 'script' of a performance lecture). Indeed, although anthologies like this—and to a certain extent, the previous work too—do not have the same character as some of the more experimental works of art writing (that experiment more formally with language or foreground process)—and there is also a limit in terms of the editors still being part of a certain kind of art/curatorial world—their inclusion of different modes of writing (especially fiction), their use of other registers besides writing (especially in terms of demarcating contents) and, once again, the performative nature of some of the writing, means they are different to academic business-as-usual and have much in common with the art writing I have already discussed (as well as gesturing back to the theory-fiction of writers like Donna Haraway and Anna Tsing who, as I have previously mentioned, have partly opened up this particular genre of writing). Certainly these books evidence the fact that a different style and presentation of writing is a necessary part of the work of any writerly contributions to decolonisation when this includes attention to the non-human also.

YWY, Searching for a Character Between Future Worlds (Sternberg). *YWY* is a collection of materials connected to the artist (and editor of the book) Pedro Neves Marques and their series of films concerning the fictional character of the book's title. The publication and films alike involve explorations of the themes of 'gender, ecology and science fiction' (Neves 2021). The book consists of essays (by invited contributors), conversations, scripts from the films, manifestos and poems—alongside film stills—all gathered together by Neves Marquez as part of their research into the above themes. In fact, the book moves away from the idea of a single-authorial intention, specifically in the way it shares the invented fictional character amongst its contributors and, for example, allows the character—or, at least, the actor playing the character—to have as much say as the artist. Here it is definitely a case of fiction 'speaking back' to its progenitors (which means it is more akin to my characterisations of art writing than theory-fiction). More generally, the book is a sustained meditation on different kinds of futurism and especially the connection of these to non-Western ontologies, such as perspectivism and animism. As far as this goes it is also, crucially, a book about the power of fiction to address these themes, especially the extractivism and other colonial disasters in Brazil.

Once again, then, it is the different styles of the various writings and their different forms of presentation—as well as the overall design by ATLAS Projectos in Lisbon—that means the book is more than just a theoretical account of the themes and issues mentioned above. The conversations especially foreground the importance of dialogic thinking in relation to decoloniality; and, more generally, the inclusion of manifestos alongside fictions means the book is also performative in some senses (insofar as the manifesto form calls for something else besides reading). Also crucial is an emphasis on storytelling as epistemic mode of knowledge production (which relates to some of what I laid out about the importance of storytelling in my essay on theory-fiction) and, with that, the importance of not collapsing indigenous accounts of the world (where, for example, there can be an identification between a people and their land) to our own subject/object system of thinking.

But how can we perform this other way of thinking from within our own? One of the contributors to this book, Marisol de la Cadena, suggests it must be through a practice of some kind, but that it might be that a certain use of words can also allow this. As de la Cadena suggests, we must 'force languages to impossibilities and alter grammars throughout' (de la Cadena 2021: 28). The book itself does not push this experimentation with language and grammar, but rather experiments more generally with form in terms of its presentation as a book. But it does suggest that formal experimentation might be part of a project of decolonisation (in terms of presenting other epistemologies from within our own).

Although—as with the previous two volumes I have discussed—this one is linked to an external practice (or is part of that practice), it nevertheless works self-sufficiently, as it were, as a book of different forms of writing (or, put differently, it presents different written inflections on its subject matter). It also reflects a key proposition of my own book: that different thematics and problems require different modes of address, not least fictional ones (or those that blur any real/fiction binary). More generally, fiction, in its different guises, can aid the project of decolonisation insofar as it turns away from what is to explore what might be (so a logic of the 'as if' again) as well as connecting to pasts that are no longer directly accessible due to colonial interruptions in the passing on of stories and other knowledges. To say it once again, fiction can present a scene of difference within the same (or operate as a kind of optical device onto that other scene). This is not to say that fiction, or for that matter art writing, is the most important aspect of decolonisation. There is a political struggle that needs to happen at the level of material reality (and, in relation to my own situatedness, in relation to institutions such as the University). But it is to say that fiction can be a resource in the imagining of the world otherwise.[48] This is even more the case when there is a performative character to this fiction, as when it calls to be performed or enacted in some manner (as, for example, with the films that this book is situated in relation too).

Important also is what might be called the meta-theme of *YWY*, which relates to some of what I have written about autofiction and autotheory in my previous essay. This is not only to assert the importance of situated knowledge (in terms of autotheory), but also the importance of interrogating the notion of the self and of the single self-conscious human agent that is often seen to exist separate from its world (this is also reflected in the book's interest in the figure of the android and AI). In many ways then this work of art writing (if it can be accurately called as such) performs its content in a further manner insofar as it plays out the explosion of this restricted category of the author/subject that is itself linked to a Western and colonial mentality. More generally—and, once again, linked to a key theme of my own book—this kind of project foregrounds (and in this case critiques) what I have been calling the fiction of the self.[49]

Notes

1. The first person to name art writing as a specific genre, at least in the UK, is Maria Fusco who also set up the first MA in Art Writing at Goldsmiths, University of London. See Fusco's own definitions and demarcations of art writing in Fusco 2011 (and the interview that in part reflects on the field in Fusco and Sharatt 2018). For examples of her own art writing, see the texts linked to at http://mariafusco.net/writing/. The MA at Goldsmiths closed in 2013, but there is now an MA (in simply 'Writing') at the Royal College of Art (headed up by Jeremy Millar) and an MLitt art writing programme at The Glasgow School of Art (developed and led by Laura Haynes), which also publishes the anthology on art writing *The Yellow Paper* (Haynes [Edbrook] 2019). For a recent gathering of art writing (understood here—to quote the anthology's subtitle—as writing 'at the intersection of writing and visual art') see Prototype's anthology *Intertitles* (Chandler et al. 2021). For some further recent definitions of art writing and a gathering together of writing *on* art writing (especially in relation to crisis, both in art writing and the world at large), see *Art Writing in Crisis* (Haylock and Patty 2021). For an earlier gathering of art writing and, once again, writing on art writing (specifically in relation to independent and self-publishing) see *Put About: A Critical Anthology on Independent Publishing* (Fusco and Hunt 2004) and *Again,*

A Time Machine: From Distribution to Archive (Everall and Rolo 2012) which, as the subtitle suggests, attends specifically to 'circuits of practice that have materialised in form of books, writing, magazines, language, spoken word, performative research and archival practice' (Everall and Rollo 2012). The Fusco and Hunt edited collection, alongside Fusco's journal *The Happy Hypocrite* (Fusco 2008–21), helped stake out the expanded field of art writing in the UK (as well as giving attention to immediate precursors and adjacent scenes of writing). The Everall and Rolo volume presents a number of essays on art writing as well as examples of such (sometimes in the same essay).

2. See, for example, the Special Issue of the journal *Art History* on 'Creative Writing and Art History' (Grant and Rubin 2011) or David Hickey's essays collected in *Air Guitar* (1997).

3. See the essays and other material gathered in the anthology mentioned in the note above—*Put About: A Critical Anthology on Independent Publishing* (Fusco and Hunt 2004)— which offers up a genealogy—and gives some contemporary examples—of the artist's book.

4. Or, to turn to more contemporary examples, there are visual art practices that use writing or text in and as their art (as with Fiona Banner or Mark Titchner, for example).

5. See, for example, the different experimental works annually longlisted for the Republic of Consciousness Prize that celebrates experimental works of literature.

6. To quote Burroughs from 'The Cut-Up Method':

   At a surrealist rally in the 1920's Tristan Tzara the man from nowhere proposed to create a poem on the spot by pulling words out of a hat. A riot ensued wrecked the theatre. Andre Breton expelled Tristan Tzara from the movement and grounded the cut ups on the Freudian couch.

   In the summer of 1959 Brion Gysin painter and writer cut newspaper articles into sections and rearranged the sections at random. *Minutes To Go* resulted from this initial cut up experiment. *Minutes To Go* contains unedited unchanged cut ups emerging as quite coherent and meaningful prose. (Burroughs 1963)

7. I will turn more than a few times to Berridge's important work (and quote him more extensively in the notes to the section on 'Sites, Scenes and Discursive Communities'), which itself offers up a series of compel-

ling definitions of and propositions about art writing. As well as these and the many descriptions he gives of different works of art writing— that he encounters at a residency at X Marks the Bökship—it is also the way his book attends to its own style and presentation and has the feel of a performance (with the bookshop as his stage set) that marks it out. Is it then also an autofiction? To quote Berridge (on being asked whether his residency will end with a performance): 'Repeated use of theatre, staging, script and character suggests a figure, an actor, who is a way of representing the sum of all these publications, which would also constitute a form of autobiography' (Berridge 2013: 77).

8. Another key figure and antecedent here is Angela Carter, who combines auto-writing, folklore, speculative fiction and so forth with formally experimental prose. See, for example, her novel *The Infernal Desire Machines of Doctor Hoffmann* (1982) or the collection of short stories *The Bloody Chamber* (1979).

9. And, for example, in the revised edition of that book—published by RE/ Search in San Francisco—Ballard provides notes and his own meta-commentary alongside the original text.

10. See also the extended discussion of Ballard and Smithson in *Fictioning* (Burrows and O'Sullivan 2019: 126–133).

11. Some of what follows—especially in the second section ('Pitch, Process and Performance') and the eighth ('Sites, Scenes and Discursive Communities')—is indebted to conversations with Tom O'Sullivan.

12. Chapman is, for myself, one of the pre-eminent practitioners of that art writing which attends to process (and, indeed, image production). See, for example, his *The Ring Mechanism* (2004) and *Diagrams for Seriality* (2014) and the collaborations with Ola Ståhl (another fine exponent of art writing), for example 'BLOODPOLLENCRYSTALSTAR' (Chapman and Ståhl 2010). Ståhl also edits and publishes experimental writing as part of Publication Studio Malmö (see especially the *In Edit Mode* series of volumes [details here: http://olastahl.com/ps-malmo/])

13. See the discussion of Acker along these lines in Burrows and O'Sullivan 2019: 43–46.

14. Hagen is also a published poet, see his collection *Lemon in Orbit* (2021).

15. In terms of the British Poetry Revival, not only are there authors that are directly associated with art writing (for example, Paul Buck or Stewart Home), but also, more generally, there is an attention to how text and image work together on the page and in a book (see, for example, the

publications of Maggie O'Sullivan) and also—in relation to some of my comments in the sections that follow—in the turn to small and often radical presses and other modes of distribution away from mainstream publishers (as, for example, in the continuing series of chapbooks produced by the poet J. H. Prynne). As with some of my other comments in this essay, there is another and more detailed account to be written about the history of art writing in relation to this more general poetic modernism of the UK. Thanks to Tom O'Sullivan for conversations around this point.

16. Thanks to Ellie Gray for bringing Lispector's writing to my attention, specifically in relation to art writing (and, indeed, automatic writing too).

17. See also the essays collected by Theo Reeves-Evison and Jon K Shaw in *Fiction as Method* (2017) and the editor's Introduction.

18. See also the editor's Preface to *Intertitles*:

> If society itself is an imaginary ensemble of practices, beliefs and truths that we subscribe to and therefore constantly reproduce, in the pages of this book you will find the overwhelming suggestion that other social organisations and interactions can be imagined. (Chandler et al. 2021: xi)

19. Thanks to Ola Ståhl for introducing me to the idea of the book as 'social object' and, more generally, for pointing out the importance of the physicality and process of manufacture of the artist's book.

20. Book Work's charity registration statement reads: 'Book Works is a registered charity, dedicated to advance education for the benefit of the public in the visual arts, particularly books which may be recognised as works of art in their own right'.

21. There is another history and genealogy to be written here around artist book design and, indeed, the distinct work of different independent designers. Again, thanks to Tom O'Sullivan for conversations around this point.

22. I mentioned Bucknall's project in my essay 'On Theory-Fiction'; here's the reference again: https://www.newmystics.xyz/

23. Although not a publisher of art writing, there is also Robin Mackay's Urbanomic, which, as well as works of philosophy and theory-fiction also publishes art books and comics (and where attention to detail in the production of a book is crucial). Urbanomic publishes other works of

theory-fiction that lean into art writing, for example, Jake Chapman's text works (see also Chapman's *Meatphysics* [2003]).

24. Fitzcarraldo also publishes two books by Paul B. Preciado (2020 and 2021) to loop back to a key author in my previous chapter on autowriting; as well as Alice Hattrick's *Ill Feelings* (2021).

25. As Berridge remarks in relation to the importance of these sites of production and dissemination:

> I wonder how texts at X Marks the Bökship are changed by their appearance in its context. They become experienced through an expanded and particular phenomenology of reading: one that emphasises different relations of text and design, different modalities of reading foregrounding performance and social event. (Berridge 2013: 31)

26. A couple of further examples in London are Burley Fisher Books in Haggerston and Donlon Books in Broadway Market (as well as BOOKS in Peckham for zines).

27. Hence also the importance of Self-Published Artist's Book Fairs.

28. To quote Berridge:

> I: Reading publications at the Bökship I find a sociable writing often taking the form of play scripts, with stage directions that make propositions about space, characters and relationships.

> J: These texts might be staged on a spectrum between full theatrical production and poetry reading or combine such sociability to their shape on the page and private reading. (Berridge 2013: 8)

29. See also the various events, reading groups and so forth identified by Waidner in their subjective history of art writing (Waidner 2021b).

30. See also Slater's writings with Jason Skeet as part of TechNET, for example the text archived here: https://datacide-magazine.com/wp-content/uploads/TechNet_insert_smaller.pdf. TechNET also presented at the *Virtual Futures* conference I mention in my essay 'On Theory-Fiction' and their presence—and flyers—were a key component of the scene of that conference.

31. I offer up this account not to write myself into this survey, but to switch to a more auto style of writing—at least to some extent—and so as to relate some of what I have written in these essays to a particular situated practice. In terms of Plastique Fantastique what follows is, of course, my

own take on that 'performance fiction' and certainly not to be taken as a definitive account (the other members of Plastique Fantastique would no doubt give different accounts). But I do want to take the opportunity here to thank David Burrows, Vanessa Page and Alex Marzeta especially for their collaboration which alongside anything else has taught me so much about art practice (and art writing), from the inside as it were. For an archive of Plastique Fantastique's work, see www.plastiquefantastique.org

32. Plastique Fantastique texts are archived here: https://www.plastiquefantastique.org/text.html

33. Plastique Fantastique performances are archived here: https://www.plastiquefantastique.org/performances.html

34. The stories—'Earth Year Zero'—were commissioned by Mikey Georgeson for 'Blake Fest' and are available here: https://issuu.com/morningdrawings/docs/earth_year_zero

35. In relation to Plastique Fantastique and in terms of theory-fiction, David Burrows and I have also recently collaborated on an essay 'Science Fiction Devices', which involves looking to various Science Fictions as method (and device), but also deploys a theory-fiction method itself (Burrows and O'Sullivan 2022).

36. See: https://www.plastiquefantastique.org/performance35.html

37. See: https://www.plastiquefantastique.org/installation15.html

38. A similar point might be made in relation to the pedagogical practices of the university. If decolonisation remains at the level of the content of various courses but does not impact on the way in which these are structured and, indeed, taught (which, once again, can repeat and reinforce various hierarchies and power structures), then it will remain ineffective in terms of any decolonisation. As well as changes in reading lists and a diversification of teaching staff, a different kind of pedagogical practice or set-up seems crucial. An example here—one I pointed to in my first essay, 'On Theory-Fiction'—is the call for collective Black Study by Harney and Moten (2013).

39. See David Burrows's *Fictioning Devices* for a development of this idea in relation to cosmotechnics and cosmopolitics (Burrows 2025).

40. I leave it to others to look to experimental writing that has its site of production away from the West and, indeed, to reflect on whether art writing could ever be an appropriate term for this writing (or even if experimental writing is a correct term).

41. I want to thank Sarah Dornhoff for introducing me to this book in a workshop at Goldsmiths, specifically about art writing and Decolonisation. Although what follows are my own thoughts, they are indebted to this initial encounter.

42. A more explicit example of 'book as gathering' (and one that is also an experiment in alternative knowledge production)—again from Archive Books—is *Electric Brine*, an anthology of writing 'at the crossroads of literature and cultural analysis' (Teets 2021: 13) that is itself the result of—and a component in—the collective curatorial project 'The World in Which We Occur'. The form of this book arises from its moments of production (the 'hosting of para educational experiments' [Teets 2021: 12]) and, like *An Ongoing-Offcoming Tale*, it also experiments with presentation, involving, for example, different typefaces and fonts and various diagrammatic line drawings within and behind the text.

43. And as such this project is indebted to Okwui Enwezor's groundbreaking Documenta 11.

44. In terms of the exploration of other and specifically non-Western epistemologies, see another publication from Archive Books, Pedro Neves Marques' *The Forest and the School: Where to Sit at the Dinner Table* (Neves Marques 2014). This volume offers up a collection of texts connected to Antropofagia understood as the Brazilian artistic/counter-culture movement, but also 'a philosophy, an ecosophy, no doubt fragmented and unfinished at each timely resurrection throughout the last hundred years of Brazilian aesthetic and political thought' (Neves Marques 2014: v). Another book by Neves Marques will be my third example in this coda.

45. There is more to say here about the relationship between 'practice as research' or 'practice research' and more experimental/performative modes of presentation. Certainly, within art writing, it is not always straightforward knowledge production that is at stake; or, put differently, the rubric of practice research from the Social Sciences and Humanities (as in research questions, methods and so forth) cannot always account for the more experimental texts that work differently or intervene in existing discourse in different ways. Perhaps this is simply to say that, although art practice can certainly be a form of research, it does not always fit within existing research frameworks within the Academy (although see also the footnote below).

46. *Fieldwork for Future Ecologies*, another edited volume published by Onomatopee, also addresses this question of fieldwork (and artistic methods more broadly). Like *Enfleshed* it contains different kinds and styles of writing (and foregrounds situated perspectives) alongside images and, once again, attention to font and typeface. Here the feel of the volume is very much a Fieldwork Guide rather than an academic tome. To quote the editors: 'In our project, "fieldwork" as a term and practice is re-shaped to reflect diverse ways of working across, in between and outside of disciplinary bounds' (Crone et al. 2022: 8).

47. See also *Five Heads (Tavan Tolgoi): Art, Anthropology and Mongol Futurism*, edited by Hermione Spriggs and published by Sternberg that likewise addresses extractivism in this region and is the written accompaniment to a project that involved five encounters and exchanges with artists. It is also a book that plays with presentation and the book form (Spriggs 2018).

48. In relation to this—and to two other publishers working between visual art and writing, both of which are increasingly attendant to questions of decolonisation—see Mara Coson's *Aliasing* (published by Book Works in 2018) and Bhanu Kapil's *Incubation: A Space for Monsters* (republished by Prototype 2023). Neither of these are explicitly—or politically/theoretically—orientated against colonialism, but both involve a different voice/narrator situated away from any dominant subject position and also, it seems to me, an exploration (and explosion) of the fiction of the self. They also involve the laying out of what might be called alternative myth-systems (in the latter case, a feminist one). Both also experiment with plot, style and presentation (which means, although they are fiction—and examples of the more experimental work being done there—they certainly lean towards art writing). This play with style and form—and with the possibilities of writing—means they relate to some of the categories I laid out in my initial definitions of art writing above.

49. See also the two books I mentioned in the footnote above.

References

Acker, Kathy (1984), *Blood and Guts in High School, Plus Two*, London: Picador.
Al-Maria, Sophia (2019), *Sad Sack: Collected Writing*, London: Book Works.
Atkins, Ed (2016), *A Primer for Cadavers*, London: Fitzcarraldo Editions.

Ballard, J. G. (1984 [1960]), *The Voices of Time*, London: Everyman.
―――― (1993 [1970]), *The Atrocity Exhibition*, London: Flamingo.
―――― (2000), 'Robert Smithson as Cargo Cultist', *Robert Smithson: Dead Tree*, ed. B. Conley and J. Amrhein, Brooklyn: Pierogi, p. 31.
Beagles, John and G. Ramsey (eds.), (2002–2016), *Uncle Chop Chop*, vols. 1-8, self-published magazine, Glasgow.
Berridge, David (2013), *Man Aarg!: Poetry, Essay, Art Practice*, London: NØ Demand at X Marks the Bøkship.
Black, Hannah (2017), *Black Pool Party*, London: Dominica/Arcadia Missa.
Burroughs, William (1963), 'The Cut-Up Method', *The Moderns: An Anthology of New Writing in America*, ed. L. Jones, New York: Corinth Books.
―――― (1969), *The Naked Lunch*, London: Transworld Publishers Ltd/ Corgi Books.
Burrows, David (et al) (2011), *Art-Writing-Research* series, volumes 1-5, Birmingham: Article Press.
―――― (2025), *Fictioning Devices*, London: Bloomsbury, forthcoming.
Burrows, David and S. O'Sullivan (2019), *Fictioning: The Myth-Functions of Contemporary Art and Philosophy*, Edinburgh: Edinburgh University Press.
―――― (2022), 'Science Fiction Devices', *New Perspectives on Academic Writing*, London: Bloomsbury, pp. 39-52.
CAConrad (2014), *Ecodeviance: (Soma)tics for the Future Wilderness*, Seattle and New York: Have books.
Carter, Angela (1979), *The Bloody Chamber*, London: Gollansz.
―――― (1982), *The Infernal Desire Machines of Doctor Hoffmann*, London: Penguin.
Chandler, Jess, A. Selby, H. Noorali and L. Talbot (2021), *Intertitles: An Anthology at the Intersection of Writing and Visual Art*, London: Prototype Publishing.
Chapman, Jake (2003), *Meatphysics*, London: Creation Books.
Chapman, Neil (2004), *The Ring Mechanism*, London: Book Works.
―――― (2010), *Glossolaris*, London: AND Publishing (Byam Shaw School of Art).
―――― (2014), *Diagrams for Seriality*, Ventor, Isle of Wight: Copy Press.
Chapman, Neil and O. Ståhl, (2010), 'BLOODCRYSTALPOLLENSTAR', *Deleuze and Contemporary Art*, eds. S. Zepke and S. O'Sullivan, Edinburgh, Edinburgh University Press, pp. 286-309.
The Confraternity of Neoflagellants (N. Hogg and N. Mulholland) (2013), *thN Lng folk 2go: Investigating Future Premoderns*, New York: Punctum Books.

———— (2021), *Pan-Pan*, New York: Punctum Books.

Coson, Mara (2018), *Aliasing*, London: Book Works.

Crone, Bridget, S. Nightingale and P. Stanton (eds.) (2022), *Fieldwork for Future Ecologies: Radical Practice for Art and Art-based Research*, Eindhoven: Onomatopee.

de la Cadena, Marisol (2021), 'Worlding Futurities: Marisol de la Cadena Interviewed by Pedro Neves Marques', *YWY, Searching for a Character Between Future Worlds*, ed. P. N. Marques, London: Sternberg, pp. 20–35.

Evans, Chris and C. Woodley (1997/1999), *STOPSTOP*, vols. 1–2, Glasgow: STOPSTOP.

Everall, Gavin and J. Rolo (eds.) (2012), *Again, A Time Machine: From Distribution to Archive*, London: Book Works.

Facey, Orion J. (2021), *The Virosexuals*, London: PSS.

Fusco, Maria (2008–21), *The Happy Hypocrite*, London: Book Works.

———— (2011), '11 Statements Around Art Writing', *Frieze*. Available at: https://www.frieze.com/article/11-statements-around-art-writing (accessed 30 November 2023).

———— (2015), *Master Rock*, London: Artangel/Book Works

———— (2018), *Dialecty* series, London: Book Works.

———— (2023), *Who Does Not Envy Us is Against Us*, Talgarreg: Broken Sleep.

Fusco, Maria and I. Hunt (2004), *Put About: A Critical Anthology on Independent Publishing*, London: Book Works.

Fusco, Maria and C. Sharatt (2018), 'Writing as a Visible Practice: An Interview with Maria Fusco', *Art and Education*. Available at: https://www.artandeducation.net/schoolwatch/229480/writing-as-a-visible-practice-an-interview-with-maria-fusco (accessed 30 November 2023).

Grant, Catherine and P. Rubin (2011), *Art History*, 34.2 (Special Issue: Creative writing and Art History).

Garnett, Robert and A. Hunt (2008), *Gest: Laboratory of Synthesis, Volume 1*, London: Book Works.

K. D. (Goldin+Senneby) (2014), *Headless: A Novel*, Berlin: Sternberg.

Goldsmith, Kenneth (2011), *Uncreative Writing: Managing Language in the Digital Age*, New York: Columbia University Press.

Hagen, Ole (2012), *Nowhere Less Now*, London: Artangel.

———— (2021), *Lemon in Orbit*, Glasgow: Pindrop Press.

Haraway, Donna (2016), *Staying with the Trouble: Making Kin in the Chthulucene*, Durham, NC: Duke University Press.

Harney, Stefano and F. Moten (2013), *The Undercommons: Fugitive Planning and Black Study*, New York: Autonomedia.

Hattrick, Alice (2021), *Ill Feelings*, London: Fitzcarraldo Editions.

Haylock, Brad and M. Patty (eds.) (2021), *Art Writing in Crisis*, London: Sternberg.

Haynes (Edbrook), Laura (2019–), *The Yellow Paper: Journal for Art Writing*, Glasgow: Glasgow School of Art.

Hickey, David (1997), *Air Guitar: Essays on Art & Democracy*, Los Angeles: Art Issues Press.

Hildegard of Bingen and H. Lemmy, with B. Kapil and A. Spawls (2020), *Unknown Language*, London: Ignota.

Home, Stewart (2010), *Blood Rites of the Bourgeoise*, London: Book Works.

———— (2002) *69 Things to do with a Dead Princess*, London: Canongate.

Inventory (D. Abbot, P. Claydon and A. Scrivener) (1995–2005), *Inventory*, No's. 1–14, London.

Jones, Nathan Allen (2022), *Glitch Poetics*, London: Open Humanities Press.

Kapil, Bhanu (2023), *Incubation: A Space for Monsters*, London: Prototype.

Kavan, Anna (2017 [1967]), *Ice*, London: Penguin.

Koskentola, Kristiina and M. van der Loo (2023) *Enfleshed: Ecologies of Entities and Beings*, Eindhoven: Onomatopee.

Lispector, Clarice (2014 [1973]), *Água Viva*, London: Penguin.

Maroto, David (2019), *The Artist's Novel: The Novel as a Medium in the Visual Arts, Part 1*, Milan: Mousse Publishing.

———— (2020), *The Fantasy of the Novel, Part 2*, Milan: Mousse Publishing.

Ndikung, Bonaventure Soh Bejeng (2022), *An Ongoing-Offcoming Tale: Ruminations on Art, Cultures, Politics and Us/Others*, Berlin: Archive Books.

Neves, Pedro Marques (2014), *The Forest and the School: Where to Sit at the Dinner Table*, Berlin: Archive Books.

———— (2021), *YWY, Searching for a Character Between Future Worlds*, London: Sternberg.

Osbaldeston, David (2015), *Inflection Sandwich*, Eindhoven: Onomatopee.

Palmer, Katrina (2010), *The Dark Object*, London: Book Works.

Pedraglio, Francesco (2021), *Battles, Vol. 1*, London: Book Works.

Perret, Mai-Thu (2008), 'The Crystal Frontier' (published in *Land of Crystal*, Zurich: JRP|Ringier).

Pester, Holly (2015), *Go to Reception and Ask for Sara in Red Felt Tip*, London: Book Works.

Phillipson, Heather (2012), *Not An Essay*, London: Penned in the Margins.

Poulson, Kit (2012), *The Ice Cream Empire*, London: Book Works.

———— (2018), *Mutter*, London: Book Works.

Preciado, Paul B. (2020), *An Apartment on Uranus*, trans. C. Mandell, London: Fitzcarraldo.

——— (2021), *Can the Monster Speak?*, trans. F. Wynne, London: Fitzcarraldo.

Priest, Christopher (2021), 'Foreword' to A. Kavan, *Ice*, London: Peter Owen. Available here: https://www.peterowen.com/christopher-priest-on-ice/ (accessed 30 November 2023).

Reeves-Evison, Theo and J. K Shaw (eds.) (2017), *Fiction as Method*, Berlin: Sternberg, 2017.

Roberts, Mo-Leeza (John Russell) (2015), *Head*, London: Book Works.

Robinson, Tom and J. K Shaw (2010–15), *Rattle: A Journal at the Convergence of Art and Writing*, No's 1-5, London.

Rowlands, Alun (2008), *Communiqué 4*, London: ICA.

Russell, John (2003–2007), *Frozen Tears*, Vols. 1-3, Birmingham: ARTicle Press.

——— (2012), 'Autonomy is Not Worth the Paper it is Written On: Writing. Written. Art-Writing. Art. Writing', *Again, A Time Machine: From Distribution to Archive*, ed. G. Everall and J. Rolo, London: Book Works, pp. 162–74.

——— (2017), *DOGGO*, ed. G. Moreno, Miami: Publications.

Scourti, Erica (2014), *The Outage*, London: Banner Repeater.

Shani, Tai (2019), *Our Fatal Magic*, London: Strange Attractor.

Slater, Howard (2012), *Anomie/Bonhomie and Other Writings*, London: Mute.

Smithson, Robert (1996a), 'The Crystal Land (1966)', *Robert Smithson: The Collected Writings*, ed. J. Flam, Berkeley: University of California Press, pp. 7–9.

——— (1996b), 'Entropy and the New Monuments (1966)', *Robert Smithson: The Collected*, ed. J. Flam, Berkeley: University of California Press, pp. 10–23.

Spriggs, Hermione (2018), *Five Heads (Tavan Tolgoi): Art, Anthropology and Mongol Futurism*, Berlin: Sternberg.

Stupart, Linda (2016), *Virus*, London: Arcadia Missa.

Stupart, Linda and C. Gent (2021), *All Us Girls Have Been Dead for So Long (A Play in Three Acts)*, London: Arcadia Missa.

Tatham, Joanne and T. O'Sullivan (1998–2001), *British Mythic*, No's 1-5, self-published magazine, Glasgow.

——— (2002), *The Slapstick Mystics with Sticks*, Glasgow: All Horizons Club.

——— (2019), *The Bitter Cup*, London: Book Works.

Teets, Jennifer (ed.) (2021), *Electric Brine*, Berlin: Archive Books.

Trecartin, Ryan (2011), 'Ryan Trecartin: in Conversation', with K. Kiamura and H. Kunzru, *Frieze*. Available at: https://www.frieze.com/article/ryan-trecartin-conversation (accessed 30 November 2023).

Waidner, Isabel (2017), *Gaudy Bauble*, London: Dostoyevsky Wannabe.

——— (ed.) (2018), *Liberating the Canon: An Anthology of Innovative Literature*, London: Dostoyevsky Wannabe.

——— (2021a), 'An Alternative Art History of the 1990s', *Frieze*, 220. Available at: https://www.frieze.com/article/isabel-waidner-alternative-90s-history-2021 (acccessed 30 November 2023).

——— (2021b), 'My Immediate Orbit: A Personal and Partial Writing-and-the-Art-World Rundown 01-21', Foreword to Chandler, Jess, A. Selby, H. Noorali and L. Talbot (eds.) *Intertitles: An Anthology at the Intersection of Writing and Visual Art*, London: Prototype Publishing, pp. xv-xviii.

Wark, McKenzie (2020), 'Girls Like Us', *The White Review*. Available at: https://www.thewhitereview.org/feature/girls-like-us/ (accessed 30 November 2023).

5

Conclusion: Four Propositions

Abstract My book concludes by briefly drawing out four general themes—or propositions—from the previous three essays that seem to me characteristic of the new kinds of writing that I have been concerned with: (1) That they work across and, in some cases, against genre; (2) That they 'perform their content' (or that style, syntax and other formal devices are crucial); (3) That different forms of collaboration (not always or only with human actors) is also often in play; and (4) That this writing is often involved in different scenes (or can even help bring these about). I end with a coda in which I reflect on the writing of this book and on the importance of constructing our own writing machines.

Keywords Against Genre, Writing as Performative, Collaboration, Writing Scenes, Theory-Fiction, Autofiction

I want to conclude this brief survey of theory-fiction, autofiction and autotheory, and art writing by drawing out four general themes—or propositions—from my three essays.

© The Author(s), under exclusive license to Springer Nature Switzerland AG 2024
S. O'Sullivan, *On Theory-Fiction and Other Genres*,
https://doi.org/10.1007/978-3-031-65072-7_5

Writing Across and Against Genre

Each of the three kinds of writing I have looked at in the preceding essays involve working across and between genre. Indeed, in many ways, the demarcations I have made—and will return to in a moment—are simply a heuristic device. Certainly, many of the writing examples that I discuss—as well as other examples of hybrid writing that I do not address in this short survey—involve the mixing up of styles and forms of presentation. A further characteristic of some of the more experimental works is that they work against genre and, as far as that goes, invent new genres too. This has implications beyond writing. As Sylvia Wynter suggests, there are different genres of the human and, as such, working across and against genre within writing is also partly to explore what the human is and can become (and in relation to this, it seems important to say that genre is only seen as such when placed against or in relation to another genre) (Wynter 1984).[1] In terms of the preceding essays, this working across genre and, with that, the construction of other kinds of device that allow for other kinds of performance—or, indeed, ceremonies—has been especially the case with theory-fiction that experiments with other perspectives and modes of expression. But it is also in play with autofiction (and autotheory) that explores genre from the other side or the inside as it were (as the 'auto' suggests). If theory-fiction can be understood as a lens or prism onto other genres of being, then autofiction operates as a mirror of sorts into the genre that we already are (although autofiction also operates as a lens into other lives too and, more generally, each of these two devices—theory-fiction as lens/autowriting as mirror—contain aspects of the other). Art writing, insofar as it involves other registers and tends to the more experimental and performative, takes this further. Might we even say that it introduces a further device into this scene of writing? Something like a multifaceted crystal that proliferates genre. Art writing is also an example of how a work can be its own singular genre (or, as Maria Fusco has suggested: 'Art Writing is re-invented in each instance of Art Writing, determining its own criteria' [Fusco 2011: n. p.]). In relation to this and to all these genres discussed in my book, there is also the foregrounding within the writing—or with the presentation of the writing—that these texts and devices are *made* things (albeit, in some cases, they are made without it being clear what their purpose might be).

Writing That Performs its Content

I mentioned the idea of writing that performs its content in my 'Introduction' to this book, and it has been one of the key themes of each of these essays. This technique/strategy is characterised by an attention to form—to style, syntax and other kinds of presentation—which is important in relation to what these different kinds of writing do, including, but also beyond, what they 'mean' in any conventional sense. It is this performing of content that also means these new genres have a different kind of traction on the world or allow us to relate to their contents in a different manner. With theory-fiction, this is especially characterised by the ways in which fiction (in whatever sense) is deployed alongside theoretical material, but also in how there can be a blurring between these different genres or regimes of sense. Even more radical is how theory-fictions can themselves be performative or take on a reality (so there is here a more general traversing across different regimes) as with the idea and practice of hyperstition. With autofiction and autotheory, although there can be writing that maintains a realist tradition—and this for good reason (concerned as this writing often is with narrating the lives of marked subjects)—there is also writing that plays with form and presentation. Writing that is, perhaps, more appropriate to the performance of the self (or of different selves). The use of an auto-style can also mean the circuits between a lived life and larger socio-economic (and ecological) factors are foregrounded. With art writing, there is a more self-conscious play and performance with different forms of representation, with the inclusion of drawings and images, for example, or the more general utilisation of different formats and layouts. But there is also the deployment of writing itself as performative, as with scripts, instructions, spells and the like. This kind of writing is then performative but also asks to be performed.

Writing, Method and Collaboration

Leading on from the above, might we also say that a different *method* is implied in some of these 'new' kinds of writing? That at stake is a different way of writing, and also a different way of approaching texts and other materials? There is, for example, the use of books and texts as objects or even props through which to enact something different in the world. Certainly it seems to be the case that reading these more performative works can operate as a trigger for our own work (and not necessarily only the written). And further, might this be a method that also foregrounds a collaborative process more generally (not least a sense of collaboration with the books and texts being looked at)? There is something about collaboration—reading and writing together—that opens things up and allows other perspectives to be taken on. These kinds of explicit collaborations also work to foreground the other collaborations we are always already partaking of and involved with. In many ways, this means that these new forms of writing ask to be treated differently—as part of a scene of writing—and, as such, we might say that alongside these new forms of writing there is also a call for new kinds of reader, too (to echo Barthes's call). My own experience of collaborative writing has often involved the interrogation of an existing self-archive (which is why it can be so challenging), but it has also involved the production of something different—a 'third thing'—that is more than the sum of its parts. A text produced by a collaboration may also have a wider valency or be somehow more open to deployment by others elsewhere. More generally, collaboration seems to be a particularly fruitful method of interacting with, if not also producing, some of the new genres of writing that have been at stake in these essays.

Writing for Communities to Come

Finally, connected to my comments above and as I also mentioned towards the end of my essay 'On Art Writing', these new genres of writing are also from (and partly for) a more general discursive community (or set of communities). Or, put differently, they are connected to different scenes of writing. There is a scene, for example, around art writing in the UK (as David Berridge has partly mapped out). There is a sense that although this scene involves a diversity of practices of writing, it is nevertheless also a 'community of singularities' (Berridge [quoting Norma Cole] 2013: 73). But besides this scene of formal experimentation and performance there is also the content of some of this writing (and here I am turning to all three of the genres I have been writing about in this short book). For example, they are often concerned with women's experience and also queer, trans and other racialised and 'marked bodies' (which themselves have a particular investment in scenes, understood as safe spaces to exist and become). As I have suggested in a couple of my essays here, this can also be broadened out to include a concern with multispecies and non-human agents and agencies (so brought into relation to the urgent issues of our Anthropocene). Another way of putting this is that this writing can foreground different and diverse worlds from within this one (just as it can foreground other perspectives on those other worlds). In many ways theory-fiction, autofiction and autotheory, and art writing can be defined against the dominance of a 'one world' thesis and its associated epistemological model and, as such, also against more major forms of writing (which can be patriarchal, hetero-cis-normative and bourgeois-extractivist).[2] Crucially, however, this refusal or turning away, as I mentioned in my second coda to the art writing essay, is also an affirmation of and turning towards other modes, styles and genres of both writing and living. Indeed, to say it once again, these last two are connected: practising and proliferating new genres of writing (when this also includes reading this writing) is also to experimentally explore these other genres of living, some of which are already here but others of which are yet to come.

Coda: On Writing Machines and Other Devices

This short book does not partake of the new genres it writes about. Indeed, in many ways, it proceeds through the more typical genre of the academic essay or monograph (albeit shorter than the latter), not least in terms of being sole authored. It is not a theory-fiction, unless that term is used to also cover works about theory-fiction (or works that gather together different examples of theory-fiction). It is not a work of autofiction or autotheory, although I have brought in some of my own investments and a more personal standpoint in the codas to my essays and in some footnotes. It is also not art writing. It does not experiment with form and presentation beyond some small gestures in that direction. Nor does it constitute its own genre as such (although it does emerge from a scene of sorts). Although not a form of machine writing—I have resisted the temptation to collaborate with ChatGPT to write my final postscript (to jump ahead a little)—it has been written on the screen and has involved a form of 'patchworking' to use Kenneth Goldsmith's term for the 'new' technique of writing that follows from word processing and the web (Goldsmith 2011: 3). Indeed, the method of writing—as I think with more or less all writing today—has been partly determined by a collaboration with machines.

On the other hand, this short book is the result of a collaboration with many individuals and books and writing practices; it is part of a wider discursive community that in many ways it attempts to both partake of and map out. I think there is also a performative aspect to what I have presented here. As well as an opportunity to think through some theoretical propositions, it has also operated as a gathering together of materials in order to enact something else. But what is that? Looking back now that I have come to the end, it is as if I have been building a platform of some kind. Or, at least, assembling components so as to build some kind of structure or, to switch metaphors, a machine—or further kind of device—which will then allow something else to take place (or, at least, come into focus): the writing of a different fiction of the self perhaps? Or the performance of a different mode of existence? Perhaps even the summoning of another community? As well as being a concern of my own book, it is also this that seems at stake in some of the writing in these new genres—that they gesture towards these other fictions, modes and communities.

For myself, this construction project is also retroactive in some ways, as it comes after the work of auto/theory-fiction that in a sense prompted it (the book *The Ancient Device* that I mentioned in one of my first notes [2024a]). It's not exactly that the present book is a reflection on that prior one, but there is a kind of theoretical reverse-engineering going on and a sense of an auto-enquiry, at least of a kind. *The Ancient Device* is a fiction about the relationship of performance to self-transformation and the fiction of the self (especially my own); but looking back, it was also about enacting or further enabling this transformation in some manner. The other collection of essays, written at more or less the same time as those here—*From Magic and Myth-Work to Care and Repair* (2024b)—also concern this fiction of the self and, indeed, other devices that might operate besides or beyond it (or disrupt it). As well as drawing on my own experiences within different worlds, those essays also looked to other practices, especially performative ones and, again, those involved in self-transformation in some manner (or with accessing other spaces and places, if not a more radical 'outside'). The essays in this book have been focused on writing more specifically—and on certain new and experimental genres in the arts and critical humanities—but insofar as any self is written it has also been concerned with what I think is one of the key devices of any project of self-transformation. After all, if a self has been written then it can be rewritten. It seems to me that these new genres of writing offer case studies and valuable resources—or further devices—for this kind of radical pursuit.

But I hope this has been more than a narcissistic project and that it might encourage you to further explore some of these other genres and writings that I have briefly surveyed. Certainly the experience of reading these other genres is different to reading writing written on them. Perhaps some of what I write might also encourage you to experiment with your own writing practices, whether that be theory-fiction, autowriting, art writing or indeed machine writing. Building your own platforms. Assembling your own devices and writing machines. Once again, this experimentation is not just literary but will necessarily implicate the fiction of the self that does that writing, as well as summon other agents and entities that will then speak back and tell you something about where they are from (and, perhaps, where they want to go). I think that it is this—the summoning of different worlds and those other fictions that are appropriate and adequate to those worlds (and allowing them to speak back to us)—which is also often a key motivation for experimenting with genre and writing, but that this can also be in play when reading theory-fiction and other genres too.

Notes

1. It's crucial to differentiate this affirmation of a diversity of genres of the human from the more right-wing assertion of 'human biological diversity', which is simply a by-word for scientific racism and its hierarchies. Wynter's account turns away from the biocentrism of race, affirming instead the things in common between different genres or what might be called our common humanity (defined by her as our ability to self-determine or 'auto-institute'). In her essay on 'The Ceremony Found' (1984), she calls for new ceremonies—as well as for a critical perspective on existing stories and narratives—that would allow for or foreground this cross-genre point of view and practice.
2. See David Burrows's critique of the one world thesis (and concomitant affirmation of many worlds) in relation to his own account of fictioning devices in *Fictioning Devices* (Burrows 2025). David Burrows and I will be further exploring this terrain in our forthcoming *Fictioning Community: The Non, the Ill and the Dead in Contemporary Art and Philosophy* (2026).

References

Berridge, David (2013), *Man Aarg!: Poetry, Essay, Art Practice* (London: NØ Demand at X Marks the Bökship.

Burrows, David (2025), *Fictioning Devices*, London: Bloomsbury, forthcoming.

Burrows, David and S. O'Sullivan (2026), *Fictioning Community: The Non, the Ill and the Dead in Contemporary Art and Philosophy*, Edinburgh: Edinburgh University Press, forthcoming.

Fusco, Maria (2011), '11 Statements Around Art Writing', *Frieze*. Available at: https://www.frieze.com/article/11-statements-around-art-writing (accessed 17 November 2023).

Goldsmith, Kenneth (2011), *Uncreative Writing: Managing Language in the Digital Age*, New York: Columbia University Press.

O'Sullivan, Simon (2024a), *The Ancient Device*, Charmouth: Triarchy Press.

——— (2024b), *From Magic and Myth-Work to Care and Repair*, London: Goldsmiths Press.

Wynter, Sylvia (1984), 'The Ceremony Must Be Found: After Humanism', *Boundary*, 13.1: 19–70.

6

Postscript: On Machine Writing

Abstract In a postscript to my book, I look at what I call 'machine writing' and especially recent Artificial Intelligence (AI) writing programmes that work from prompts. I also briefly attend to some precursors to this scene—earlier experiments with algorithmic writing and other theoretical accounts of post-conceptual and post-internet writing. I am interested in what these new forms tell us about writing more generally and, perhaps, what has always already been in play with it (for example, that there has always been an inhuman aspect). Connected to this is also the way in which these AI systems open up debates about what intelligence is or could be. As such, these systems operate as devices, which, as well as anything else, offer up a perspective on our own form of intelligence (and on what it means to be human), but also on those other forms—or genres—of non-human intelligence that already surround us (and, in this sense, machine writing, like the other kinds of writing I have explored in my book, has a performative aspect, albeit more obliquely in this case).

Keywords Machine Writing • Artificial Intelligence • ChatGPT • Theory-Fiction • Non-Human Intelligence • Fictioning

© The Author(s), under exclusive license to Springer Nature Switzerland AG 2024
S. O'Sullivan, *On Theory-Fiction and Other Genres*,
https://doi.org/10.1007/978-3-031-65072-7_6

Introduction

In this postscript to my three essays I want to briefly look at what might be called 'machine writing', understood as a particular kind of human–machine collaboration or what David Burrows and I have elsewhere called 'mythotechnesis'.[1] I have in mind here especially recent Artificial Intelligence (AI) writing programmes—or 'large language models'—that work from written prompts, but, more generally, AI systems that are involved in generating representations (so those that produce images or animations from written prompts too). In my first essay 'On Theory-Fiction' I attended, albeit briefly, to earlier writing collaborations with machine systems—for example, K Alado-McDowell's *Pharmakon AI* (2020)—and in what follows I will also return to some theoretical accounts I looked at there (in particular those by Kenneth Goldsmith and Amy Ireland) that attend to how writing has changed since digitisation and the arrival of the Web (which might itself be understood as a precursor to—or at least precondition of—large language model AI). These new technologies have instigated what might be called a new genre of writing (what Goldsmith calls 'uncreative writing' [Goldsmith 2011]). On a deeper level, and following Ireland in particular, I am also interested in what these new forms of writing tell us about writing in general and, perhaps, what has always been in play with it (for example, that there has always been an inhuman or non-human aspect). Connected to this is also the way in which these AI systems open up debates about what intelligence is or might become. I would argue that they operate as devices which, as well as anything else, offer up a perspective back on our own form of intelligence (and on what it means to be human), and also on those other forms of non-human intelligence that already surround us (so different genres of intelligence, if I can put it like that). It is also in this sense that these new kinds of writings, like the others I have explored in this book, have a performative aspect to them, albeit more obliquely in this case.

Definitions

It is certainly the case that AI writing programmes like ChatGPT have surprised many of us.[2] I know I am not alone in feeling that there has been a step change in the capabilities of these systems, not least in terms of their interaction with humans. From my limited understanding and perspective, this step change is clear at the level of writing—the generation of text from prompts—but a brief survey of the literature shows that this is only the surface of the deeper problem solving that ChatGPT can accomplish (see, for example, the discussion in Bubeck et al. 2023).[3] Also impressive and surprising are the image-generating capabilities of DALL-E and, in particular, the way it produces its composite images from text prompts. That said, and although it is early days, it does seem as if this system is caught within a certain genre of image production.[4] This will, to some extent, be down to the prompts—or the users writing the prompts—but it might also signal a limit (at least for now) in terms of computer-generated images. Unlike ChatGPT, some results are also less convincing or demonstrate a limited understanding of a given prompt (no doubt this will change—as will the accuracy and precision of different representations—as we move further into an AI-determined future).

My sense, however, is that these AI systems are in fact not really involved in understanding at all (or, at least, our understanding of understanding). And, likewise, that there is not exactly an intention at work behind the text that is generated from ChatGPT, for example. Rather, at work is a logic of mimicking. We might be reminded here of Peter Watt's first-contact novel *Blindsight* (2006). The aliens—non-human forms of intelligence—in that novel do communicate, but it is clear—at least relatively speaking—that they are simply mimicking their human interlocutors. Or, put differently, they are not aware of the meaning of the words they use (although it is equally clear that there is an advanced intelligence at work).[5] Watt's book stages an encounter between these two forms of intelligence (as well as other non-human and neurodiverse set-ups). Our interaction with AI shares many characteristics of this first-contact scenario and attempts at communication.

A sense of understanding and meaning is then not necessarily at stake in our encounter with AI systems which operate by predictive algorithms coupled to very large data sets (a key characteristic of these systems is that they have a great deal of information instantly available).[6] Indeed, as users of ChatGPT, we are contributing to this AI resource, hence the increasing attention to intellectual property issues. There are various other urgent issues here, connected especially to the vast increases in computational power needed for these AI systems. Where are the servers that these AI systems are running on, for example? Who owns them? And what rare metals are being used in their manufacture—and where are they being mined from? I will leave it to others to attend to these questions, but would remark here (before going on to consider the implications for writing of these machines) that increased computational power has very real ecological and environmental implications (not least in terms of that question of extraction and coloniality that I have mentioned in previous essays).

It is the ability of ChatGPT and other AI systems to 'deep learn' (built as they are on 'deep neural networks') that then means their text generation is increasingly seamless or reads as non-machinic (as evidenced, for example, by ChatGPT's ability to conduct convincing conversations with humans). ChatGPT—built as it is on the Python programming language—can learn from its errors in what has been called 'back propagation' (so this generation of machines might be described as recursive). We have certainly passed the Turing Test and, it seems, ChatGPT-4, for example, is also now able to successfully complete the law bar exam. In my own field of work, the more readily available ChatGPT-3.5 is also able to offer up relatively convincing definitions, accounts and arguments—certainly, at the level of a very good undergraduate paper (although, as is the case with DALL-E, there does seem to be some limits to how successfully ChatGPT follows some given prompts, as evidenced by sometimes rudimentary errors or the generation of falsehoods [which OpenAI call 'hallucinations']; once again, these AI systems are less concerned with truth—or verified/verifiable facts—than with producing something convincing to their human interlocutors). ChatGPT-3.5 is also able to convincingly mimic different writing styles, again depending on the prompts given. It is this, the way ChatGPT-3.5 can change its style of writing, that for me is especially interesting (and relevant to the essays in this book)—as well as the way it can, to a certain extent at least, be creative and inventive—as it demonstrates that style (a key theme of my essays) is not a question of expression (of a given agent or subject) but an emergent quality of formal methods. Put simply, and taking a very broad view, ChatGPT further demonstrates Roland Barthes's thesis about the move from work to text and, indeed, the death of the author.

Precursors

There have been other recent writings attentive to how the death of the author has been further played out or enacted through machines. Kenneth Goldsmith's *Uncreative Writing* (2011), for example, lays out how writing—and especially creative writing practice—has fundamentally changed with the advent of various technological machines, from copiers and scanners to ubiquitous digitisation and the World Wide Web.[7] As Goldsmith suggests, it is increasingly the case that text is not produced by authors but by machines, and reading (for meaning) is no longer an adequate mode of interaction with such material (if only because there is so much of it). For Goldsmith, we are just on the edge (or were on the edge at the time of the publication of his book) of a massive paradigm shift in terms of the implications for creativity (and of what the latter actually means) of this increasing technologically determined world. To quote Goldsmith from the very end of his book: 'Uncreative writing—the art of managing information and re-presenting it as writing—is also a bridge, connecting the human-driven innovations of twentieth century literature with the technology-soaked robopoetics of the twenty-first' (Goldsmith 2011: 227).

Hito Steyerl makes an analogous argument that reproductive technology changes something fundamental in relation to the ontology of representation (or at least certain forms of representation) in relation to what she calls the 'poor image' (Steyerl 2012). For Steyerl, this has both reactionary and progressive aspects, but it is also, more generally (and as with Goldsmith's account of uncreative writing), now part of the condition of reality we live in (which is what the term 'post-internet' also names). To quote Steyerl from the end of her essay:

> The poor image is no longer about the real thing—the originary original. Instead, it is about its own real conditions of existence: about swarm circulation, digital dispersion, fractured and flexible temporalities. It is about defiance and appropriation just as it is about conformism and exploitation. In short: it is about reality. (Steyerl 2012: 44)

Both of these arguments about technology and representation—Goldsmith and Steyerl—are haunted by Walter Benjamin's writings on the loss of aura and increasing democratisation of the work of art in the age of mechanical reproduction (Benjamin 1999). They also echo some of Jean Baudrillard's ideas about the order of simulacra and the loss of the referent. Or, put differently, for both of these contemporary writers, mechanical reproduction fundamentally shifts things, for good and bad, but has also taken a further leap with ubiquitous digitalisation.

Elsewhere Goldsmith also discusses an artist whose work with texts mimics machines (so works the other way around, as it were, to ChatGPT) (Goldsmith 2014). As I mentioned in my essay 'On Theory-Fiction', Ryan Trecartin's scripts certainly involve using a kind of machine writing or, at least, terms and linguistic constructions that are either from computer speak—and coding—or that mimic its style. In some cases, Trecartin uses a kind of writing that takes this style and does something further with it (so, again, taking machine speak as its own prompt, as it were; another kind of recursion). David Burrows and I have referred to this kind of work—which might be seen as a collaboration with machines so as to produce other realities—as 'machine fictioning' (see Burrows and O'Sullivan 2019: 435–507).[8] But Goldsmith also makes the argument that these developments might be seen as part of a 'tradition' of formal innovation and experimentation that goes back to post-war modernist writers like Gertrude Stein. In his book on *Uncreative Writing*, Goldsmith broadens out this genealogy to include authors like James Joyce (especially with *Ulysses* and *Finnegan's Wake*) and Walter Benjamin (especially with what Goldsmith sees as a key precursor to uncreative writing, *The Arcades Project*).

In his book *Glitch Poetics*, previously mentioned in the third essay of my book, Nathan Allen Jones also attends to the way in which 'new' technologies—and our interaction with them—have changed artistic and creative writing practices (Jones 2022). He offers up a series of contemporary case studies, some of which might be described as art writing, including examples I have also discussed like Linda Stupart's *Virus* (2016) and Erica Scourti's experiments in autowriting. The influence of technology is especially evident, for Jones, in those practices that attend to disruptions and glitches in communication and information. Or, more specifically, with those practices that stage these disruptions in different ways or use them to produce something different (the glitch being both a break in one regime of sense, and also, and at the same time, an affirmation of a different regime, perhaps even one to come).

Amy Ireland takes some of this further, making a compelling argument that these new writing technologies demonstrate a factor that is always already in play in writing and, especially, in literary avant-garde forms that work against typical sense-making (see Ireland 2017a). Writing has always been on a vector away from the human. For Ireland—following the work of Sadie Plant (discussed in my first essay)—this is also part of the secret link—or even a secret alliance?—between machines and women, insofar as both of these upset—or are set against—the property form of patriarchy (especially as incarnated in the self-possessed sovereign subject) (see Ireland 2017b). In my essay 'On Autofiction and Autotheory', I argued that writing can be a method of foregrounding the 'fiction of the self' (or, at least, of opening up some space around it), but here, writing—from *écriture féminine* to AI-generated text—can also announce an end to some of these fictions (of the self), as well as foregrounding other agencies—and other fictions—that are situated away from the human.

Non-human Intelligences

There are things we associate with human intelligence that ChatGPT at the moment cannot achieve; but, on the other hand, the latter also demonstrates—in the similarities—something about how our own intelligence, especially in terms of language use, operates. As I have suggested elsewhere, there is something about building a model—if we can go along with the idea that AI is a model of sorts—that then allows a perspective back on the model we already are (the 'fiction of the self' again) (See O'Sullivan 2024). It's difficult to get a perspective on this fiction. We cannot step on our own shadow. But by turning in the other direction and building a representation, a further kind of recursive knowledge (of the fiction of the self) becomes possible. I would not claim that this is the most important aspect of AI. Rather that it is a kind of side-effect that has implications for our understanding of ourselves and, indeed, for how we understand our collaboration with these machines.

There is more to say here in terms of the debate on whether these AI systems really are intelligent (or soon to become so)—or, indeed, what intelligence actually is (not least in relation to those other and different human neurodiverse setups)—but there is also a bigger picture or, at least, a wider context to consider. Simply put, there are other forms of intelligence already out there that are irreducible to the human (and especially the historically specific one of the Modern Western subject). We humans do not have the monopoly on intelligence and, indeed, our own definitions and yardsticks are invariably caught up with various value systems and judgements. This also means that there are racialised logics in play in our account of what intelligence is. These logics play out in the biases of AI systems (after all, they are made by—and trained on—us),[9] but might it also be the case that our attitude to AI—as a different form of intelligence—also plays out some of these deep racialised structures and hierarchies (as demonstrated by some of the fears of the machine uprising, robot rebellion and so forth).

So here there is a further secret alliance drawn between machines and other non-human intelligences, in particular, animals.[10] After all, the latter, too, tend to be subordinated to our own intelligence (hence that extractive attitude—treating the non-human as resource for the human—that, once again, I have mentioned in a couple of my previous essays). To evaluate and judge these other forms of intelligence only against the yardstick of human intelligence (which, as I mentioned above, is always already informed by various hierarchies and power relations) is to have always already captured them in pre-existing interpretive frameworks and, indeed, to subordinate them to a kind of human ideal. Both animals and AI will always be less than this ideal (as will we).

Just as there are ongoing experimental human collaborations with machines—in terms of writing—the same is true with animals. In 'On Theory-Fiction', I briefly looked at some accounts of written theory-fictions about inter-species animal collaborations and sympoiesis (especially in Donna Haraway's work), but two examples of more direct collaboration are Vinciane Despret's account of the communication skills of Hans the horse (2004)—I will return to this in the following section of my essay—and Laura Cull Ó Maoilearca's account of her research involvement in a performance project by the performance group Fevered Sleep, *Sheep Pig Goat* (2019).

Is there a limit here in terms of writing and, indeed, representation? On one level, it does not seem that animals inhabit a symbolic universe in the same way as humans (in Burroughs's terms, they have not caught the language virus). Nevertheless, it has long been accepted that some species communicate through gesture and signs. And then, like AI systems, animals can and do mimic our communication systems—as an interface with us. As with AI, it is also clear that their intelligence—when that term is not restricted to the symbolic—surpasses our own in many ways. Might it also be that in order to 'understand' these other intelligences we will need to learn how to interface with them or adapt ourselves to their own systems of expression (so change our own attitudes and perspective as it were)? Certainly, we must be careful not to approach them only on our own terms or reduce their intelligence and modes of expression to our own already-existing understandings and interpretive frameworks.

Who Is Mimicking Whom?

This is partly the argument of the Despret article mentioned above, which concerns the horse Hans who was able to accurately answer mathematical questions posed to it by humans through tapping its hoof. As Despret points out, it is the way in which Hans's human interlocutors adapt their minimal muscular movements (only picked up on under close investigation) so that the horse can 'read' them—as in the communication of 'zero' not with an ellipsis, but with a shake of the head—that means, ultimately, it is the horse prompting and teaching its human questioners how to communicate (and not the other way around). To quote Despret:

> How could it happen that humans replace their own spontaneous movements with that of the horse, unless we assume that Hans taught them the gestures he needed? Hans has made them move otherwise, he changed the habits of their bodies and made them talk another language. He taught them how to be affected differently in order to affect differently. (Despret 2004: 116)

Hans, we might say, was teaching his human interlocutors a sign system—a form of writing—that would allow him to then comply with their desires (insofar as, more generally, Hans exhibited a 'preference for agreement' [Despret 2004: 116]). In Ó Maoilearca's terms, this was a 'reciprocally transformative interspecies encounter' that was enacted through 'embodied empathy' (a couple of phrases she uses in relation to her account of the performance I mentioned above [2019: 4, 2]).

To say it again, rather than Hans simply mimicking us humans, we are involved, at least partly, in mimicking Hans. Something like this is also at play in relation to machines in Goldsmith's account of humans copying text or mimicking technological processes (which is, in part, his definition of 'uncreative writing'). In their article 'Secrets and Machines: A Conversation with GPT-3', Ethan Plaue and William Morgan offer up a further compelling take on this idea of reverse mimicry (Plaue et al. 2023). Their essay—written in collaboration with ChatGPT-3—gestures towards a kind of 'anti-messianism' implicit in AI: the way in which it heralds the death of God (and a certain attendant regime of meaning) and, following that, the opportunity for a new collaborative relationship with machines (so, again, a form of mythotechnesis). But for my specific purposes at this point in my essay, it is the way in which the machine implicitly demands that our prompts are 'understandable', which means we will invariably become more machine-like ourselves. Or, to quote Plaue and Morgan at length:

one could assert that in order to talk to our machines, we must teach ourselves to speak the languages they understand. Speaking to the next generation of machines will require us to talk as if we were a bit more machinelike
ourselves. But this raises something troubling…who is really mimicking
whom? If our response to GPT-3 is indeed to machine our speech in order
to prompt it to more accurately produce what we desire, then perhaps the
proverbial shoe is on the other disembodied foot. Here, we are not the
mimicked, but instead the mimickers of our machines. They are the ante-
rior originators of our mimicry; it is *they* who prompt *us* into our becoming-
machinic. (Plaue et al. 2023: n. p.)

Or, put differently, the machines—like the animals we communicate
with—are teaching us how to write *for them* so that they might act and
respond appropriately (in terms of meeting our desires and so forth).

More generally, and following N. Katherine Hayles on this point, it is
then not as if there is a large gap or difference between us and machines
or animals in terms of this other intelligence. All of us are involved in
what Hayles calls non-conscious cognition (which is also what Hans the
horse demonstrates in his pattern recognition and other processes of
'understanding'), albeit with humans, this is interfaced with conscious
and unconscious thinking too (Hayles 2017). In relation to machines
specifically, all of us humans are also increasingly involved in a symbiotic
relationship with these new technical systems. Or, again, as Hayles has
argued, we humans are involved in a co-evolution with machines in a
process she calls technogenesis (Hayles 2012).[11] Writing is one form of
connection and communication between us and machines. It's not the
only one—there are other forms of call and response, other forms of
interaction and, again, possible collaboration—but it is the one that
allows the most sophisticated communication. Or, put another way, writing is a key mediating device between different kinds and forms—and
again, genres—of intelligence. Crucially, this is not a one-way street.

Future Fictions

To return to AI and its future—which is also our future—a brief survey of some of the literature (including from mainstream media sources) suggests two opposing poles in play, with different takes attached to one or the other. On the one hand, there are critiques of AI, ranging from those who see in it all sorts of serious biases carried over from human society (see, for example, Gray 2023, Bridle 2023 and Amaro 2022) to those who see it as just the latest gambit and land grab by the elites, whatever the rhetoric and promises of a utopian future (see Klein 2023).[12] Related to these positions are also those laments that always tend to occur in relation to technological development and its impingement on the human.[13] And then there are also those that see these technological developments in AI as a very real existential threat to human existence, if not life in general (see Yudkowsky 2023). On the other hand, there are those who see AI development as emancipatory and as more or less the next phase in human and post-human evolution (for example, promising an escape from our existential finitude)—or, more extreme, that see humans as merely an early chapter in the adventure of intelligence that is inevitably continued with machines. One example, on the far edge of this extreme, is the 'Right accelerationism', expounded by Nick Land, for whom the human is simply a kind of pollinating insect for the larger and more complex AI systems that are actualising themselves from the future. For Land, this 'techonomic' process is synonymous with capitalism.[14] On the other edge of this tendency, there are writers like Reza Negarestani who see the evolution of AI (or, more especially, AGI, Artificial General Intelligence) as part of a left-leaning 'labour of the human'—again, the continuing self-actualisation of intelligence—which is ultimately emancipatory in character (Negarestani 2018). There are other less extreme takes here that nevertheless see AI as having the potential to solve all sorts of human problems and crises (as well, more generally, as alleviating drudgery). All of these are fictions about the future and are even, to some extent, theory-fictions.

But, of course, these are not the only accounts of what the future holds. Accompanying AI developments—and perhaps partly foregrounded by them—is the increasing awareness of those other intelligences and agencies I mentioned above. It is this growing awareness of other intelligences that seems increasingly characteristic of our time (and our attendant visions of the future). AI is just one example of this non-human intelligence and agency, albeit one that we have set the initial conditions for. There is a competition of sorts here between capitalist development (which can mean positioning these other agencies and non-human intelligences as resources [if not simply exterminating them]) and a non-capitalist mode which involves detaching from a certain sense of progress/ growth and profit motivation—and accompanying extractive mentality—and pivoting in another direction, perhaps towards care and repair, not least for the diversity of non-human intelligence and life (and, indeed, for the planet in general).[15] Between these two are those Left accelerationist accounts that envisage mobilising the platforms of capitalism (of which AI is already a key example) towards non-capitalist aims. Again, these different accounts might be understood as theory-fictions and, as such, they can be understood to be involved, at least partly, in attempting to bring about the reality of the visions they present (they are hyperstitional or work as 'sociopolitical attractors' in this sense).[16]

Following this Left accelerationism and situated between the various positions of utopia and dystopia I mentioned above—or at a tangent to them perhaps—there is something more like an attitude of experimental collaboration with machines (as well as with other non-human intelligences). There is an openness, here, to what new 'universes of reference' this kind of collaboration can open up (again, this is what Burrows and I have called 'mythotechnesis'). Yuk Hui develops just such an argument in his recent article on 'ChatGPT, or the Eschatology of Machines' where he suggests that narratives to do with the singularity—whether utopian or dystopian—are part of an eschatological thinking that stymies a more valuable and pragmatic understanding of the 'prosthetic function' of machines (and especially recursive machines such as ChatGPT) and how the latter might play a part in 'realising human potential' (Hui 2023: n. p.). Along the way, Hui develops his own account of 'machine intentionality' away from the tendency to anthropomorphise, affirming instead a more general 'biodiversity, noodiversity, and technodiversity' (Hui 2023).

Progressive developments in art and culture more generally do not arise from a turning away but rather a turning towards and utilising of new technology, even if—especially if—that technology is used contrary to any initial intended function (so untethering technologies from capitalist logics and protocols, perhaps). It is for this reason that mythotechnesis is often found in the realm of contemporary art practice. Writing, broadly conceived, has a role to play here too—not only in the speculation about these future collaborations but also in the enacting or performing of them (when this means a collaboration with writing machines, too). This is, then, a writing about the future that also helps call different futures forth.

Conclusion

To conclude this postscript, I want to return to writing and to the question of genre that has been in play in all of the essays gathered here. Machine writing certainly announces a new genre in one sense—or even, as I suggested above, a number of new genres (after all, collaborations often work at the edges of existing genres and gesture towards those to come). But in another sense—in the way, for example, in which AI can mimic any and all genres—machine writing also announces the end of genre, when the latter is tied to the expression of an all-too-human agent. But is there, hidden within this, something else at work? Something that is no longer concerned with the genres of the human, but, perhaps, with the genres of the non-human (those that are here but including those that are yet to come)? And might it be that we are already in a process of learning (or mimicking) these other genres? Certainly, to repeat the point I made above, collaboration with other agents and agencies allows other, perhaps stranger genres to take shape. It is this, ultimately, that links this new form of writing to those others I have written about in my previous essays. Following Amy Ireland, perhaps it is right to say that machine writing is simply the latest form of writing in an ongoing adventure: one in which any sole human intention (or fiction of the self) can only ever have been a chapter. This is an adventure which might well be towards the stars, but which is also involved in exploring—and collaborating with—the more proximate non-human intelligences that already surround us. It is in this sense, once again, that writing—and especially those examples of it that cross genre or work from outside given genres—are inextricably linked to other modes of existence, some of which are to come, but many of which are already here.

Notes

1. We use this term to describe very particular human–machine collaborations that are involved in what we call fictioning, understood here as the instantiation of other realities within this one (see Burrows and O'Sullivan 2019). In terms of a more technical definition of machine writing, I should also say that, in the following essay, I am not concerned specifically with coding or algorithms as forms of machine writing nor with other accounts of the culture of software. For a discussion of the latter, see Fuller 2017; for a discussion of the ingress of computation into culture, see Parisi 2013. Nor am I concerned with any detailed accounts—or fictions—of and around any machinic singularity (although in relation to the latter, see Burrows and O'Sullivan 2019: 397–415).

2. ChatGPT is produced by Open AI, a not-for-profit (initially, at least) organisation whose stated goal is to achieve human-level intelligence (or AGI, Artificial General Intelligence).

3. Although this is not to take only a celebratory tone. New AI systems might well be highly effective at problem solving, and they may well indicate a brighter future, but only if untethered from the private and corporate interests whose key motivation is profit. I briefly go into the different utopian/dystopian takes on AI below, but for a recent takedown of some of the utopian promises and myths of AI development, see Naomi Klein's Guardian article 'AI machines aren't "hallucinating". But their makers are' (Klein 2023).

4. Although see also the example of digital cryptids—for example 'Crungus' and 'Loab'—that can be produced by prompts (these are images/entities that 'speak back' to their progenitors—or prompters—as if they came from elsewhere). Is this a further form of hyperstition? Certainly, it's a case of fiction taking on a reality (or, at least, an actuality).

5. See also the description of these large language model AI systems as 'stochastic parrots' (parrot in the sense of parroting a word or phrase [repeating without a sense of meaning] and stochastic, suggesting random probability) (Bender et al. 2021).

6. And these data sets contain biases which invariably leads to biases in the AI text generation.

7. See also definitions of the genre of 'electronic literature', which, at least in part, follow from the way computers allow for hyper-text links (and, in relation to this, see also my discussion of Sadie Plant's *Zeros and Ones* in 'On Theory-Fiction' and the brief comment about the use of QR codes in the discussion of Bejeng Ndikung's *An Ongoing-Offcoming Tale* in the second coda to my essay 'On Art Wrtiing').

8. Related to this is also the practice of 'digital storytelling', itself related here to the increasing availability of digital recording and editing software (not least on phones and other mobile devices). Although it has not been the concern of this essay there is also the way different Social Media platforms have themselves instituted 'new' and different genres of writing (the blog post, tweet, and so forth). And then there are also those theory-fictions that operate in and across social media and other digital platforms, such as 9MOTHER9HORSE9EYES9. For a discussion of some of these and, more generally, a critical survey of artistic writing practices impacted by 'new' technology (so another kind of machine or 'performance writing') see Nathan Allen Jones' *Glitch Poetics* (2022).

9. For a discussion of the racialised biases of AI (and especially facial recognition systems) see Ramon Amaro's *The Black Technical Object* (Amaro 2022).

10. Plants are also increasingly seen as having their own intelligence and/or as operating as active agents within a milieu. In terms of plant intelligence and the present essay there is, again, K Allado-McDowell's *Phamako-AI* which as well as being a collaboration with a non-living intelligence—ChatGPT—is also a sustained meditation on non-human life and especially plants (and on biosemiotics). We might also understand other features of our world as forms of non-organic life, broadly understood. Certainly, there is a sense that rivers, for example, have their own way of being and even an agency of sorts—having also been granted legally recognised personhood in some states. More clear is that they need our care and, in some cases, repair too.

11. See also the fuller discussion of technogenesis in relation to fictioning in Burrows and O'Sullivan 2019: 435–440.

12. For James Bridle, this is not the only issue with AI. A more important one is that it blurs distinctions between truth and reality. Bridle is also especially alert to the issue of ownership, and what he suggests is the 'primitive accumulation'—of the commons of the internet—by tech corporations for profit (what he calls the 'enclosure of the imagination') (Bridle 2023). Although Bridle makes the argument that AI is stupid and merely collages together already existing images, he does write about AI cryptids or composite forms that are, as it were, fictioned by AI systems. As I mentioned in note 4, it seems to me that there is something interesting here about machine–human collaboration that can produce images that 'speak back' as if from another place. Bridle is also attentive to the way AI systems can be made to work against corporate tech culture, as, for example, when gathering, revitalising and disseminating threatened indigenous languages. For Bridle, then, the issue is not the technology, but the capitalist profit motive that dictates its direction and use.

13. See, for example, Franco Berardi's essay 'Unheimlich: The Spiral of Chaos and the Cognitive Automaton' (2023), which warns of the dangers, especially of 'self-learning automated devices' that are concerned not just with executing tasks (or means) but also in establishing goals (or ends). For Berardi, this signals a new threat, but is also part of the more general alliance between automation and chaos (especially apparent within resurgent Nationalisms) that produces panic and defines the 'animal' that is 'strangling humanity'. For Berardi, then, the opposition here is between intelligence and consciousness, where the former 'is the ability to win the game thanks to combinatory ability' and the latter involves 'ethical and aesthetic reflection about the goals of the game' (Berardi 2023: n. p.). Ultimately, consciousness, for Berardi, is to exist in time (or, more simply, to experience). It is the 'sense of living in the horizon of death…this is not translatable into recombinatory language' (Berardi 2023: n. p.). Berardi's account is part of that scene (if I can put it like that) that is intent on preserving the human as a special category over and against machines (and might we even say also other forms of life?). In fact, such accounts are themselves part of a larger opposition that values the natural—or the given—over the manmade (see Ray Brassier's account of accelerationism as partly reversing this structuring binary and asserting a Promethean impulse over a religious one [Brassier 2014]).

14. To quote Land from one of his more theory-fiction texts:

> The story goes like this: Earth is captured by a technocapital singularity as renaissance rationalization and oceanic navigation lock into

commoditization take-off. Logistically accelerating techno-economic interactivity crumbles social order in auto sophisticating machine runaway. As markets learn to manufacture intelligence, politics modernizes, upgrades paranoia, and tries to get a grip. (Land 2011: 441)

15. I explore this expanded idea of care and repair further in my book *From Magic and Myth-Work to Care and Repair* (O'Sullivan 2024).

16. See Alex Williams's linking of this idea of attractors back to the Ccru idea of hyperstition that I discussed in my first essay:

> as regards political accelerationism, what becomes crucial is the ability of a reconstituted Left to not simply operate inside the hegemonic coordinates of the possible as established by our current socioeconomic setup. To do so requires the ability to direct preexisting and at present inchoate desires for post-capitalism towards coherent visions of the future. Necessarily, given the experimental nature of such a reconstitution, much of the initial labor must be around the composition of powerful visions able to reorient populist desire away from the libidinal dead end which seeks to identify modernity as such with neoliberalism, and modernizing measures as intrinsically synonymous with neoliberalizing ones (for example, privatization, marketization, and outsourcing). This is to invoke the idea, initially coined by Land's Cybernetic Cultural [sic] Research Unit, of hyperstition—narratives able to effectuate their own reality through the workings of feedback loops, generating new sociopolitical attractors. This is the aesthetic side of the task of constructing a new sociotechnical hegemony. (Williams 2013: 9)

References

Amaro, Ramon (2022), *The Black Technical Object: On Machine Learning and the Aspiration of Black Being*, Berlin: Sternberg.

Benjamin, Walter (1999), 'The Work of Art in the Age of Mechanical Reproduction', trans. H. Zohn, *Illuminations*, London, Pimlico, pp. 211–44.

Bender, Emily M. , T. Gebru, A. McMillan-Major and S. Shmitchell (2021), 'On the Dangers of Stochastic Parrots: Can Language Models Be Too Big?', *FAccT '21: Proceedings of the 2021 ACM Conference on Fairness, Accountability, and Transparency*, pp. 610–23. Available at: https://dl.acm.org/doi/10.1145/3442188.3445922 (accessed 24 August 2023).

Berardi, Franco (2023), 'Unheimlich: The Spiral of Chaos and the Cognitive Automaton', *e-flux*, March 10 2023. Available at: https://www.e-flux.com/notes/526496/unheimlich-the-spiral-of-chaos-and-the-cognitive-automaton (accessed 24 August 2023).

Brassier, Ray (2014), 'Prometheanism and its Critics', *#Accelerate: The Accelerationist Reader*, ed. R. Mackay and A. Avanessian, Falmouth: Urbanomic, pp. 469–87.

Bridle, James (2023), 'The Stupidity of AI', *The Guardian*, 16 March 2023. Available at: https://www.theguardian.com/technology/2023/mar/16/the-stupidity-of-ai-artificial-intelligence-dall-e-chatgpt (accessed 24 August 2023).

Bubeck, Sébastien, et al (2023), 'Sparks of Artificial General Intelligence: Early experiments with GPT-4', arXiv:2303.12712v5. Available at: https://arxiv.org/abs/2303.12712 (accessed 25 August 2023).

Burrows, David and S. O'Sullivan (2019), *Fictioning: The Myth-Functions of Contemporary Art and Philosophy*, Edinburgh: Edinburgh University Press.

Cull Ó Maoilearca, Laura (2019), 'The Ethics of Interspecies Performance: Empathy beyond Analogy in Fevered Sleep's *Sheep Pig Goat*', *Theatre Journal*, 71.3: E-1–E-22.

Despret, Vinciane (2004), 'The Body We Care For: Figures of Anthropo-zoo-genesis', *Body and Society*, 10.2–3: 111–134.

Fuller, Matthew (2017), *How to be a Geek: Essays on the Culture of Software*, Cambridge: Polity.

Goldsmith, Kenneth (2011), *Uncreative Writing: Managing Language in the Digital Age*, New York: Columbia University Press.

——— (2014), 'Reading Ryan Trecartin', *Lizzie Fitch/Ryan Trecartin: Priority Innfield*, London: Zabludowicz, pp. 91–7.

Gray, Chantelle (2023), 'AI Ethics and Biases, and the Mindlessness of Deep Learning', *University World News*, 19 April 2023. Available at: https://www.universityworldnews.com/post.php?story=20230419154324393&fbclid=IwAR1DGgySGgFt3_30Lh4DBjzDpLclsFL1ZwQRCIq213c6B_nJfPkWh6x-V1Hk (accessed: 8 June 2023).

Hayles, N. Katherine (2017), *Unthought: The Power of the Cognitive Unconscious*, Chicago: University of Chicago Press.

——— (2012), *How We Think: Digital Media and Contemporary Technogenesis*, Chicago: University of Chicago Press.

Hui, Yuk (2023), 'ChatGPT, or the Eschatology of Machines', *e-flux*, 137. Available at https://www.e-flux.com/journal/137/544816/chatgpt-or-the-eschatology-of-machines/ (accessed 24 August 2023).

Ireland, Amy (2017a), 'The Poememenon: Form as Occult Technology', *Urbanomic Documents*. Available at: https://www.urbanomic.com/document/poememenon/ (accessed 5 September 2021).

Ireland, Amy (2017b), 'Black Circuit: Code for the Numbers to Come', *e-flux*, 80. Available at: https://www.e-flux.com/journal/80/100016/blackcircuit-code-for-the-numbers-to-come/ (accessed 5 September 2021).

Jones, Nathan Allen, (2022), *Glitch Poetics*, London: Open Humanities Press.

K Allado-McDowell (2020), *Pharmakon AI*, London: Ignota.

Klein, Naomi (2023), 'AI machines aren't "hallucinating". But their makers are', *The Guardian*, 8 May 2023. Available at: https://www.theguardian.com/commentisfree/2023/may/08/ai-machines-hallucinating-naomi-klein (accessed 24 August 2023).

Land, Nick (2011), 'Meltdown', *Fanged Noumena: Collected Writings 1987–2007*, eds. R. Mackay and R. Brassier, Falmouth: Urbanomic/New York: Sequence, pp. 441–59.

Negarestani, Reza (2018), *Intelligence and Spirit*, Falmouth/New York: Urbanomic/Sequence Press.

O'Sullivan, Simon (2024), *From Magic and Myth-Work to Care and Repair*, London: Goldsmiths Press.

Parisi, Luciana (2013), *Contagious Architecture: Computation, Aesthetics, and Space*, Massachusetts: MIT Press.

Plaue, Ethan, W. Morgan and GPT-3 (2023), 'Secrets and Machines: A Conversation with GPT-3', *e-flux*, 121. Available at: https://www.e-flux.com/journal/123/437472/secrets-and-machines-a-conversation-with-gpt-3/ (accessed 24 August 2023).

Stupart, Linda (2016), *Virus*, London: Arcadia Missa.

Steyerl, Hito (2012), 'In Defence of the Poor Image', *The Wretched of the Screen*, Berlin: Sternberg Press, pp. 31–45.

Watts, Peter (2006), *Blindsight*, New York: Tor.

Williams, Alex (2013), 'Escape Velocities', *e-flux*, 46. Available at: http://www.e-flux.com/journal/46/60063/escape-velocities (accessed 17 November 2023).

Yudkowsky, Eliezer (2023), 'Pausing AI Developments Isn't Enough. We Need to Shut it All Down', letter in *Time*, March 29 2023. Available at: https://time.com/6266923/ai-eliezer-yudkowsky-open-letter-not-enough/ (accessed 24 August 2023).

Index[1]

---

[1] Note: Page numbers followed by 'n' refer to notes.

© The Author(s), under exclusive license to Springer Nature Switzerland AG 2024
S. O'Sullivan, *On Theory-Fiction and Other Genres*,
https://doi.org/10.1007/978-3-031-65072-7

SPRINGER NATURE

GPSR Compliance

The European Union's (EU) General Product Safety Regulation (GPSR) is a set of rules that requires consumer products to be safe and our obligations to ensure this.

If you have any concerns about our products, you can contact us on ProductSafety@springernature.com

In case Publisher is established outside the EU, the EU authorized representative is:

Springer Nature Customer Service Center GmbH
Europaplatz 3
69115 Heidelberg, Germany

The manufacturer's authorised representative in the EU is Springer
Nature Customer Service Centre GmbH, Europaplatz 3, 69115 Heidelberg,
Germany. If you have any concerns regarding our products, please
contact ProductSafety@springernature.com

Printed and bound by CPI Group (UK) Ltd, Croydon, CR0 4YY

24/04/2026

02096315-0015